BAD LAW

BAD LAW

Rethinking Justice
for a Postcolonial Canada

John Reilly

Emily
Welcome to my
veew of the Law
John Reilly

RMB

For information on purchasing bulk quantities of this book, or to obtain media excerpts or invite the author to speak at an event, please visit rmbooks.com and select the "Contact" tab.

RMB | Rocky Mountain Books Ltd.
rmbooks.com
@rmbooks
facebook.com/rmbooks

Cataloguing data available from Library and Archives Canada
ISBN 9781771603348 (paperback)
ISBN 9781771603355 (electronic)

Printed and bound in Canada

Front cover: adapted from a painting by Stoney artist Roland Rollinmud

We would like to also take this opportunity to acknowledge the traditional territories upon which we live and work. In Calgary, Alberta, we acknowledge the Niitsitapi (Blackfoot) and the people of the Treaty 7 region in Southern Alberta, which includes the Siksika, the Piikuni, the Kainai, the Tsuut'ina and the Stoney Nakoda First Nations, including Chiniki, Bearpaw, and Wesley First Nations. The City of Calgary is also home to Métis Nation of Alberta, Region III. In Victoria, British Columbia, we acknowledge the traditional territories of the Lkwungen (Esquimalt, and Songhees), Malahat, Pacheedaht, Scia'new, T'Sou-ke and WSÁNEĆ (Pauquachin, Tsartlip, Tsawout, Tseycum) peoples.

We acknowledge the financial support of the Government of Canada through the Canada Book Fund and the Canada Council for the Arts, and of the province of British Columbia through the British Columbia Arts Council and the Book Publishing Tax Credit.

Disclaimer
The views expressed in this book are those of the author and do not necessarily reflect those of the publishing company, its staff or its affiliates.

For Sean (1970–2016)

❖

CONTENTS

INTRODUCTION

We can't solve problems by using the same kind of
thinking we used when we created them.
— Albert Einstein

When I was a young lad the term colonialism was a romantic word that conjured up visions of courageous people going out into the wilderness, clearing land for farms and building towns in desolate, forbidding locations. These colonial people were to be admired and respected for their sacrifices, which ultimately enabled future generations to live here in comfort and prosperity.

The early years of white settlement among the Indigenous people had some advantages for the Indigenous people. The fur trade allowed them to use their hunting and trapping skills to obtain tools and weapons made from metal, which was something they didn't have before the coming of the colonials.

But as time went by things became very bad for the Indigenous people. Diseases the colonials brought, to which they had no immunity, wiped out millions, and as the Indigenous population diminished, the colonial population grew, and eventually the leaders of the new immigrant society decided they wanted to have total control of the Indigenous population. This they took through treaties which the Indigenous people did not understand, and through the use of reserves, residential schools and the Indian Act, which controlled every aspect of the First People's lives.

Now, the word colonialism has a much different meaning for me. It is the meaning that the Indigenous people have given it for years. It is a word that describes the process by which a foreign immigrant society took control of their lives and destroyed their freedom.

One of the worst aspects of colonialism was the forcing of a foreign system of law upon the Indigenous people. If we, the non-Indigenous people, are going to be truly postcolonial, and truly seek reconciliation, I suggest we should think about adopting their system for ourselves.

My learning in this regard started in the 1990s when I began to inquire as to why there were such disproportionate numbers of Indigenous people appearing in the courtroom where I presided as a judge. What I learned completely changed my thinking about our justice system.

The criminal justice system in Canada, and much more so in the United States, is a mess – the courts are backlogged, cases are dismissed because they can't be heard in a reasonable time, and there are frequent complaints about inconsistent sentencing and overcrowding in prisons.

From my experience of 40 years in the criminal justice system, 33 of them as a judge in the Provincial Court of Alberta, Criminal Division, I see the system as out of control and doing more harm than good.

The solutions call for more judges, more lawyers, more police, more court workers, and the list goes on.

I experienced national and international notoriety in the mid-1990s because of judgments I wrote, and actions I took, to try to improve the delivery of justice to the Indigenous offenders in my jurisdiction.

The media referred to me as "the controversial judge," "the fighting judge," "the renegade judge," "the outlaw." ("Renegade judge" was the one my friends on the "rez" liked best.)

I changed the way I thought about justice, and in doing so I believe I applied Einstein's advice, even though I didn't think of it that way at the time.

The change began with my efforts to understand why there was such a disproportionate number of Indigenous people appearing in the court where I presided.

Indigenous elders talk about "wisdom stories," the events of their lives that taught them about living and gave them wisdom. This book is the third part of my own wisdom story.

I told the first part of my story in *Bad Medicine: A Judge's Struggle for Justice in a First Nations Community*. I spoke of the cases and the people that influenced my thinking about Canada's relationship with its Indigenous people. The book is the story of the change in my thinking about our so-called justice system

I told the second part of my story in *Bad Judgment: The Myths of First Nations Equality and Judicial Independence in Canada.* That book recounts my conflicts with the court administration which were the result of my efforts to apply the law to Indigenous people in a culturally sensitive way.

This, my third book, tells of my dream. My dream of a system that uses the vast resources of the criminal justice apparatus to improve social conditions amongst the people of Canada, a system that helps wrongdoers live better lives instead of just throwing them away by locking them up. It is a dream of a utopian system, but I believe it is a real possibility if only people could see that peace does not come from punishment.

The focus on the punishment of wrongdoing is wrong. If the money and effort that is devoted to punishment were devoted to social betterment, our society would be a better, safer, more peaceful place in which to live.

My experience with Indigenous elders is that they almost never say to a person "you should do this" or "you must do that." Rather they will say "this is my experience, and this is how I see it." They leave it to their listener to take whatever lesson they will take. I have found this gentle way of teaching to be a part of the charm that has so endeared them to me.

It is not my nature to be so gentle, but it is my intention in writing this book to describe my experience, and tell how it changed my thinking, in the hope that I might influence the thinking of my readers, and that my readers might change their thinking in relation to justice and in relation to the plight of the Indigenous people of this country.

❖ I ❖

THE BEGINNING

The journey of a thousand miles begins with the first step.
— Lao Tsu, *Tao Te Ching*

When I began sitting as a judge, I was starry eyed about our glorious justice system. I saw it as a system that levelled the playing field for rich and poor, protected the innocent and punished the guilty. I now see that younger self of mine as hopelessly naive.

I maintained that view for about the first 20 years of my career. I performed my judicial duties about the same way I did my work in law school. There, you learn what the professor wants to hear, you put that in your papers and you do well. As a judge I learned what the Court of Appeal wanted to hear, I put that in my judgments and I did well. That is, if you think the Court of Appeal agreeing with you is doing well. I got to the point where I thought I was doing better when they disagreed with me. I recall a fellow judge saying: "Even when the Court of Appeal agrees with me, I sometimes still think I'm right."

I look back on my early years and shake my head at the thought of the young judge, with basically no life experience, making decisions that had profound impact on the lives of the people he dealt with. I think my saving grace was that I was usually inclined to err on the side of leniency. Also, I don't like bullies. As a young lawyer I appeared before judges whom I would categorize as bullies. Men who were so authoritarian that appearing before them was always unpleasant. I remember a conversation with Ed McCormick, a legendary criminal lawyer who was still practising when he was in his 80s. He asked me how long it would take for me to develop "judge-itis" (the unfortunately arrogant demeanour that many jurists develop when they are elevated to the lofty position of the bench). I assured Ed I never would, and I believe I can safely say that I always tried to exercise the power of my office with respect for those appearing before me.

From the time I was appointed until 1993, I sat in the Criminal Division of the Provincial Court in Calgary. From 1981 to 1986 I was assigned as the circuit judge, travelling from Calgary to the towns of Cochrane, Airdrie and Didsbury. Those five years gave me my first experience with Aboriginal offenders. All of the charges on the Stoney Indian Reserve at Morley require the accused to appear in the court in Cochrane.

The reserve covers approximately 400 square kilometres, with Cochrane on its eastern edge, the Kananaskis River on the west. It includes land north of the Bow River and south of the Trans-Canada Highway. About 3,000 people were living on the reserve in the mid-1990s, while the population of the entire area serviced by the court in Cochrane was about 30,000. So the reserve made up about 10 per cent of the total population. Usually about 80 or 90 per cent of the court docket was made up of cases from the reserve.

I was seeing Indigenous people at their very worst. I saw the violence and the alcoholism in a very forceful way. I read hundreds of presentence reports, which are prepared by probation officers in serious cases. In one the accused's father had been murdered. In another the accused's father was serving time for murder. Many others recounted deaths of relatives by suicide or in fatal accidents. The picture of dysfunction and despair that these reports presented made it difficult to imagine how the accused before me could have done anything else than commit the offence he had committed. I saw them at their worst and yet I saw something endearing about them.

I remember a case in which a man was charged with assault occasioning bodily harm. I presided at his preliminary hearing, a procedure in which my function was only to determine whether there was sufficient evidence to order the accused to stand trial. The allegation was that he hit the victim with a weight from a barbell set. The victim testified that the offender had come up behind him and as he turned around, he was struck with the weight and lost consciousness.

The defence lawyer cross-examined the victim on his ability to make the positive identification.

> So, you say that you turn around, and you're hit with this barbell and knocked unconscious, but in that split second before you lost consciousness you are able to identify this man as the man who hit you?
> Yes.
> Had you ever seen him before?
> No, but I had seen a picture of him.
> Where did you see that picture?
> In his wife's bedroom.

I looked at the accused and he looked back at me. He kind of winked and nodded. It was like he was saying. "Yeah, I did it, but he deserved it." I ordered him to stand trial, even though I was tempted to dismiss the charge. The accused didn't think he had done anything wrong, and in the circumstances I was inclined to agree.

Another time, he got drunk and in a jealous rage he broke a beer bottle and cut his wife's face with it. He pleaded guilty to that charge, and in speaking to sentence his victim/wife asked me not to send him to jail. I told her she should leave him, that it would be good for her to be rid of him. I told her this was an offence that called for three years in the penitentiary. She pleaded with me not to give him federal time, that at least if I gave him provincial time he could serve it in Calgary and she could go there to visit him. So I gave him two years less a day.

I saw the woman at a meeting at Morley a few years later. I asked her how she was doing and if they were still together. She said they were and she thanked me for giving him the shorter sentence. She didn't think the imprisonment had done any good, but he was attending AA and staying sober, and life was okay.

He had taken treatment, and alcohol counselling had done some real good. It is unlikely the imprisonment did any good at all.

The last time I saw him was at a funeral at Morley. It is a tradition at Morley to have a reception line at the end of a funeral, and members of the tribal council will be part of the line. He had been elected to council, and we shook hands as I went down the reception line. I don't know how he feels about me all these years later, but he shook hands with me, and he does seem to be doing okay.

Another case I remember from the '80s was an assault matter in which a man was caught by a police officer in the act of beating his wife. She was on the ground and he was kicking her in the face. Apparently he had given her money to buy a bottle of wine. She purchased the wine and then drank the bottle before going back to meet him.

The Crown's first witness was the police officer. His evidence alone was more than sufficient to establish the charge against the accused, but the Crown also called the wife. She was one of the most pathetic people I ever saw in my courtroom. She shuffled up to the witness stand. The clerk asked her to take the oath to tell the truth and her answer was barely audible. The Crown then asked the usual question: "On such and such a day something happened to you that brings you to court. Please tell us about it."

The accused glowered at her and she made an inaudible reply. She was asked to repeat what she said. Her answer was, "I deserved it."

The accused did not testify and I don't recall his lawyer making much argument about the inevitable conviction. I surmise the not guilty plea had been entered in the hope that the trial would not proceed.

Unfortunately, many of the cases of domestic assault were dismissed because witnesses did not show up to testify. I suspected this was often because they were intimidated. This particular case did not depend on the victim's testimony, of course, because the police officer had actually witnessed the offence. I found the accused guilty, and in view of the viciousness of the assault, I sentenced him to three years in a federal penitentiary.

The case may have been the beginning of my doubts about the concept of specific deterrence – the legal theory that if you punish someone for an offence, they will not repeat the offence because they will not want to incur further punishment.

Two years after I sentenced him, he was released on mandatory parole, having served two-thirds of his sentence. The day he was released he got drunk and drove out to her house to settle the score. Fortunately the woman barricaded herself in the house and phoned the police. He was so enraged that he drove his car into the side of the house. He was arrested and appeared in court the next day.

His wife was in court and she stood up and said she had received counselling while he was in prison and she was no longer willing to submit to his violence. The only benefit the criminal proceeding accomplished had been to give the woman the opportunity to get help, but it was obvious it had done the man no good at all.

I don't know what subsequently happened to him. Having already convicted and sentenced him, I was required to recuse myself from further matters in which he was involved.

I didn't always disqualify myself from subsequent cases involving an accused I had dealt with. I had a number of people who became familiar with me because of repeat charges of public intoxication, and I would glibly sentence them to 30 days. Sometimes I would tell them: "This is not to punish you, it's to give you a chance to dry out before you kill yourself."

In *Bad Medicine* I tell the story of Ken Soldier, whom I had sentenced to imprisonment many times for public intoxication before I sentenced him to a treatment-oriented penalty. He took the treatment and remained sober for the rest of his life. He even served a term as chief. It is one of a few success stories that make me think my work as a judge was not completely wasted.

The change in my thinking about justice began with what I saw in relation to Indigenous offenders, but then I also saw that the inadequacies of the system applied to virtually all those who appeared before me,

At 30 years of age I was the youngest person ever appointed to the Provincial Court of Alberta. I was far too young to be exercising the powers and responsibilities of judicial office, but when I compared myself to some of the crotchety old men I worked with, I often felt I was doing a huge service to those people who came before me. I was saving them from the far worse fate they would have faced had they appeared before some of my colleagues.

I don't think my youthfulness made me any less able to make the decisions I was required to make, but my lengthy career gave me the opportunity to take a long and critical look at the justice system. It was a learning experience that involved a growing awareness of the plight of the Indigenous people and the difficulties they faced in the justice system.

One of the most important lessons I learned was the concept of "worldview." For the first time in my life I realized that not everyone sees the world the way I do, and this changed the way I see the world.

My favourite example is the forest. I love to walk in the mountains and when I was younger I liked to build things like fences and decks. As I walked through the forest I would look at the trees and see the 2×4s and 4×4s I could cut from them. Then I learned about the Indigenous worldview and their concept of the interrelatedness of everything in nature. Now when I walk in the forest, I see the trees breathing in the carbon dioxide that I breathe out and their breathing out the oxygen that I breathe in.

I learned that my concept of "justice" was not universally accepted, that there were different ways of dealing with wrongdoing. I learned that the Canadian criminal justice system, of which I was once so proud to be a part, did not have all the answers.

Now that I am old and retired, and no longer have to fear the sanctimonious pronouncements of higher courts or administrative judges, I am able to state my opinions more freely. Not that I was ever very restrained in my comments, but even in my most militant judgments I could hardly say that the whole system is nonsense and wastes billions of dollars that could be much better spent. Much worse than the waste of money is the waste of human lives – the lives that are destroyed by a cruel and archaic system that has its roots in the Dark Ages.

There have been efforts to improve the system over the years. We no longer use corporal punishment, but its use was only abolished as an option of judicial sentencing in 1972.

In the history of our justice system, offenders were subject to various methods of sadistic punishment, including the strap, whipping with the cat-o'-nine tails, bread and water diet, paddling, and flogging.

Only as late as 1962 were penitentiary regulations introduced in Canada restricting the use of the strap to a maximum of 15 strokes for "flagrant or serious disciplinary offences."

In 1996 the government of Canada attempted to reduce the

use of imprisonment by enacting amendments to the Criminal Code which instructed sentencing judges to consider all sanctions "other than imprisonment."

In January 2018 a B.C. court declared that administrative segregation provisions of the Corrections and Conditional Release Act were unconstitutional because they amounted to torture, created a significant risk of serious psychological harm and increased the incidence of self-harm and suicide. Following that, the Liberal government introduced legislation that will eliminate the use of administrative segregation (solitary confinement) altogether.

So, as we attempt to make punishments more humane, I ask: "Why do we use them at all?"

The immediate answer from the entire legal community will be: "deterrence." We believe that if we punish wrongdoers for their wrongdoing they will stop doing wrong (called "specific deterrence"), and potential wrongdoers will see the punishments and refrain from the wrongdoing they might otherwise do ("general deterrence").

My observation is that this doesn't work, and there have been numerous studies which support my position. The recidivism rate in Canada (people reoffending after being released from prison) is said to be one of the highest in the world, and this alone should cast severe doubt on our methods of dealing with wrongdoing.

If our objective is simply to punish because it makes us feel good, or because we have a religious conviction that tells us that people who do wrong should be punished, then we should carry on with what we are doing. However, if we truly want the just, peaceful and safe society that the Criminal Code says is the purpose of sentencing, we should think more about that goal. The imposition of "just sanctions," which the Criminal Code says is the means to achieve that end, is not the end in itself; and if it is not working, I think we should be looking for a different means to attain the goal we seek.

The purpose and principles of sentencing became law in 1996 by the following section:

> **718** The fundamental purpose of sentencing is to protect society and to contribute, along with crime prevention initiatives, to respect for the law and the maintenance of a just, peaceful and safe society by imposing just sanctions that have one or more of the following objectives:
>
> a) to denounce unlawful conduct and the harm done to victims or to the community that is caused by unlawful conduct;
> b) to deter the offender and other persons from committing offences;
> c) to separate offenders from society, where necessary;
> d) to assist in rehabilitating offenders;
> e) to provide reparations for harm done to victims or to the community; and
> f) to promote a sense of responsibility in offenders, and acknowledgment of the harm done to victims or to the community.

Prior to the passage of these provisions, there were no statutory directions for judges to follow in passing sentence. We were supposed to know the case law and decide each case on "precedents."

So, in any given case we were to look at what other courts had done in similar "preceding" cases, and do the same as the other courts had done.

The problem with this is that if the preceding courts were wrong in what they did, those errors got perpetuated by the system based on precedent.

I came to believe that the courts have been wrong for hundreds of years – that the basic error is the theory that we can achieve the goals of a "just, peaceful and safe society" by punishing wrongdoing, when there are much more enlightened ways of dealing with it.

The problem is that the system seeks to punish rather than to fix.

There is no definition for "crime" in the Criminal Code; crime is any activity that is legislated to be an offence.

An offender is defined in the Code as a person "guilty of an offence," and then there are a few hundred sections that essentially say "anyone who does this (unlawful activity described) commits an offence and is liable to (imprisonment and fines as set out)."

The objective of maintaining a just, peaceful and safe society is laudable, but the method – imposing sanctions – is archaic and counterproductive.

The order of the subparagraphs in s. 718 is indicative of the real purpose. Denunciation of the conduct and the harm done, deterrence from further offences and separation of the offender from society are the primary objectives (paragraphs a, b and c). Rehabilitation of offenders, reparation for harm done and promotion of a sense of responsibility in offenders are secondary (paragraphs d, e and f).

This is the mindset of our culture and it is unlikely to change in our lifetime, but I believe we would be much more successful in achieving the ideal of a just, peaceful and safe society if we took a different approach.

Like Martin Luther King Jr., I have a dream. I have a dream of a justice system that actually contributes to the well-being of our society by resolving conflict and promoting peaceful interactions among our people.

My experiences and my own difficulties disillusioned me to the extent that I resigned my appointment as a judge. I could no longer do what the law required of me. I could no longer impose required sentences, especially mandatory minimum terms of imprisonment, when, in my view, doing so was more immoral than the conduct that incurred the penalty.

I wrote judgments in which I attempted to apply the Indigenous justice concepts I learned. Those judgments resulted in disciplinary action against me. I was ordered to move from my home in Canmore, where I had jurisdiction over a First Nations community, back to Calgary, where I could be kept under the watchful eye of the assistant chief judge and prevented from making further pronouncements on the need to treat Indigenous offenders according to their culture.

I was ultimately vindicated. I challenged the order of transfer by commencing litigation which resulted in a judgment that declared the order to be invalid. Judgments of the Supreme Court of Canada, specifically in *R. v. Gladue*, confirmed my position that the amendments to the Criminal Code in 1996 did in fact require a different approach to the sentencing of Aboriginal offenders.

I may even have made a small contribution to the awareness which culminated in the Truth and Reconciliation Commission and in Prime Minister Trudeau's address to the General Assembly of the United Nations in September 2017 in relation to Canada's Indigenous people.

I have often been asked if I would like to see a separate system of justice for the Indigenous people. My answer is that I would rather see a system based on Indigenous justice concepts that would apply to everyone.

I have taken great comfort in the Truth and Reconciliation Commission's report, *Honouring the Truth, Reconciling for the Future*. It said many of the things I was saying in the '90s. When I said them, I was accused of a "loss of objectivity" with Aboriginal offenders, and that is why I was ordered to move out of the jurisdiction that was bringing those offenders before me.

I would like to have seen the TRC report go further than it did. I make further comment on this in chapter 26.

❖ 2 ❖

LEARNING

The Canadian criminal justice system has failed the Aboriginal people of Canada.
— Royal Commission on Aboriginal Peoples

The 1990s were a time of general awakening to the plight of the Indigenous people of Canada. At least it seemed like that to me.

In 1986 I was reassigned to the court in Calgary and until 1993 I sat mostly in the city. Then, in 1993, I had the great good fortune to be transferred to the mountain town of Canmore, to become the resident judge for Canmore and Banff.

The dockets in both towns were light, and at my suggestion the sittings in Banff were reduced and the town of Cochrane was added to the Canmore/Banff circuit. I was again the judge primarily responsible for justice on the Stoney reserve, but it was with a different perspective.

My new position as the resident judge in a small town gave me a sense of independence and responsibility that I had not experienced before. It was the beginning of a change in my thinking. I was now the judge primarily responsible for justice in my assigned area. Before this, when I was just one of twenty-some judges in Calgary, I didn't feel I had much of an impact on the system as a whole.

The greatest challenge, and the catalyst that changed my life, was of course the Stoney Nakoda reserve at Morley.

In the '80s I knew nothing about Indigenous people, and that was the wisdom of the day. A judge was supposed to be objective, so any prior knowledge of an accused person was a reason for a judge to recuse himself from a case.

In the '90s, however, there were several events that made non-Indigenous people begin to take notice of First Nations people.

In Alberta the construction of the Oldman River dam was being resisted by the Piikani Nation, specifically Milton Born With a Tooth and the Lone fighters. Although the dam eventually did get built, the controversy over it was an event that contributed to the awareness of the aspirations of Indigenous people that we had largely been able to ignore previously. (I deal with this in detail in chapter 7.)

The episode also led to the establishment of a provincial task force on the criminal justice system and its impact on the Indian and Metis people of Alberta. Their report, released in 1991, was of special interest to me because its author, the task force chair, Allan Cawsey, had been the chief judge of the Provincial Court who invited me to apply to become a judge and had guided me through the process.

Justice Cawsey said two things in that report that had a significant effect on me. One was that judges who don't know anything about the communities in which they preside are seen as judicial tyrants. The other was that treating people who are different as if they are the same is "systemic discrimination."

I took these things to heart and made an effort to get to know the people and learn about their traditions and customs.

The ironic thing is that when I started my quest, my intention was to learn enough about them that I could explain my glorious justice system to them in terms they would understand. In my naïveté I thought that if they just understood the system, they eventually would appreciate it and embrace it.

What I came to see was that they viewed our system as an instrument of their oppression, and I began to agree with them.

The justice system is just a part of the whole process of government. For Indigenous people it is part of the process that took away their traditional way of life, prosecuted them for their spiritual practices and enforced the law that required them to surrender their children to residential schools. The system so damaged their social and family structure that it was understandable they didn't see any good in it.

Other events that happened in the '90s were the Oka crisis, the defeat of the Meech Lake Accord, and the amendment to the Criminal Code that gave special recognition to Aboriginal offenders.

In July of 1990 the town of Oka, Quebec, was planning to build a golf course on land claimed by the Mohawk of Kanesatake. The Mohawk objected to the development and there was a 78-day armed standoff between them and Canadian armed forces in which a Canadian soldier was shot and killed.

The Meech Lake Accord, negotiated by Prime Minister Brian Mulroney in 1987, was a proposed constitutional agreement that would have had Quebec accept the Constitution Act of 1982 and would have recognized Quebec as a "distinct society." The accord required ratification by all provinces by June 30, 1990.

Elijah Harper, an Indigenous member of the Manitoba Legislative Assembly, prevented the passage of the accord. He objected to it because it was created with no input from Indigenous people and contained no provisions for them. He filibustered in the Manitoba Legislature for 12 days in order to prevent ratification.

These events led to the creation of the Royal Commission on Aboriginal Peoples, which released a magisterially comprehensive report in 1996. I read all five volumes.

I was upset to learn, for example, about the fraudulent creation of the treaties. The federal government of the day had promised the Indigenous people that their way of life would be preserved forever. At the same time, the prime minister, Sir John A. Macdonald, told Parliament that "the great aim of our legislation has been to do away with the tribal system and assimilate the Indian people in all respects with the other inhabitants of the Dominion as speedily as they are fit to change." The Indian Act, which took control of every aspect of their lives, had already been passed.

I was also upset to learn about the criminalization of Indigenous spiritual ceremonies. My father's family came here from Ireland to escape discrimination against Catholics. One of the great blessings of our beloved Canada was that it gave us religious freedom. To think that the same Canada took away the religious freedom of the people who were already here was troubling to me.

The information on the residential schools was the most disturbing. Children were taken away from their parents to "take the Indian out of the Indian child." Some say as many as half of them died in those schools.

I had never heard about residential schools until I attended a conference of Federation of Saskatchewan Indian Nations in the mid-'90s. One of the presenters was a woman who talked about "the schools." I asked someone what she was talking about. She looked at me like I had come from a different planet. It was the first reference to residential schools I had ever heard, and it meant nothing to me.

Thomas King in his book *The Inconvenient Indian* describes the attitude of the Canadian government in a style I find delightfully flippant. Unfortunately it is devastatingly accurate:

> The schools in both countries [i.e., the US and Canada] were, for the most part, overcrowded. Diseases flourished. Sexual and physical abuse was common. The children received neither proper nutrition nor proper clothing. In 1907 Dr. Peter

Bryce submitted a report to Duncan Campbell Scott, the superintendent of the Department of Indian Affairs, which set the mortality rate for Native students at residential schools in British Columbia at around 30 per cent. The rate for Alberta was 50 per cent. I'm not sure exactly how Scott reacted to the report, but, in 1910, he dismissed the high death rate at the schools, insisting that "this alone does not justify a change in the policy of this Department, which is geared towards the final solution of our Indian problem."

Final solution. An unfortunate choice of words. Of course, no one is suggesting that Adolf Hitler was quoting Scott when Hitler talked about the final solution of the "Jewish problem" in 1942. That would be tactless and unseemly. And just so we're perfectly clear, Scott was advocating assimilation, not extermination. Sometimes people get the two mixed up.

In 1919 Scott abolished the post of medical inspector for Indian agencies. Perhaps the position fell to budget cuts. Perhaps Scott and his department were still stinging from Bryce's report and decided that the best way to deal with mortality figures was not to keep them.

By the time I read the RCAP report I was 50 years old, had been a judge for 20 years and had never heard about one of the worst atrocities ever committed in Canada.

Indigenous people who engaged in spiritual ceremonies, and those who tried to keep their children out of residential schools, could be prosecuted in the Canadian criminal justice system. The system was thus an instrument of their oppression, and learning this totally disillusioned me.

Some relief came in the 1996 amendments to the Criminal Code, and I particularly embraced this provision:

> **718.2**(e) all available sanctions other than imprison-
> ment that are reasonable in the circumstances should be

considered for all offenders, with particular attention to the circumstances of aboriginal offenders.

There was no question in my mind that the Canadian criminal justice system had failed the Indigenous people and it was necessary, in the name of justice, that steps be taken to rectify this.

❖ 3 ❖

GETTING TO KNOW THE STONEYS

Oh, that is so wrong. You make decisions that will affect a per-
son's life forever and you can't even know those people?
— Rose Auger, Cree Medicine Woman

In *Bad Medicine* I tell of some of the people who influenced my thinking:

Jeff Williams, a log-home builder. When I complained about the difficulty I was having in getting to know the Stoneys, he said to me: "John, we took their land, they don't like you."

Marjorie Powderface, an Indigenous court worker who named her adopted son Riley in my honour. She told me that if I wanted to do something to help the Stoneys, I should start by going to the Eagle's Nest, the women's shelter on the reserve.

Tina Fox, the director of the Eagle's Nest. Elected to the tribal council in 1996, she supported me in my efforts to expose political corruption and financial mismanagement on the reserve. One of the most powerful lessons I learned was from her. She told me she was attending a healing circle for a young man who had killed her niece in a fatal car accident. I recognized his name from the court docket. In her world, she prayed for him. In my world we would punish him. I liked hers better.

Rose Auger, a Cree Medicine Woman, introduced me to the sweat lodge and told me: "We won't cook you, we will teach you how to pray." When I told her I could not have her son's case transferred to my court so I could sentence him, because I couldn't be objective, she said: "Oh, that is so wrong. You make decisions that will affect a person's life forever and you can't even know those people?"

John Snow, United Church minister, recipient of two honorary doctorates from the University of Calgary, chief of the Wesley band of the Stoney Tribe from 1970 to 1992 – The Reverend Doctor Chief John Snow. When I asked him if we could work together to design programs that would help his people, he told me there was no funding available and just "blew me off." My information was that the tribal income for 3,500 people was over $100-million, but there was no funding for alcohol treatment or anger management. I formed a very negative opinion of John Snow.

Ernest Wesley, chief of the Wesley band from 1992 to 1996, during which time he had done some tremendous work with education. Unfortunately, when he was again elected in 2000, he seemed to have gone over to the dark side – preoccupied only with consolidating his power and maintaining the divisions in the Stoney Community.

The Stoney are divided into three groups: the Wesley, the Chiniki and the Bearspaw. They used to refer to themselves as three "bands" making up the Stoney "tribe." Now they call themselves the Wesley First Nation, the Chiniki First Nation and the Bearspaw First Nation.

In my opinion this division of the community is a huge impediment to social development. The only reason for it seems to be the selfishness of the men who want to be a chief. Each would rather be a chief of one of the divisions than risk not being elected to the one position.

In my effort to get to know the Stoney, I often picked up hitchhikers when I was driving across the reserve. One day I picked up Tom Amos, a former chief. He told me he had no doubt that the Stoney were one people before the treaty and that the three bands were a creation of the treaty, but he was adamant that if they did not have three chiefs they would lose their treaty rights.

It is ironic and very sad that these divisions are perpetuated by the current chiefs, but they began with the policy of Canadian colonialism. Canada divided the First Nations because the divisions made the people weak and easier to control so that they would be easier to assimilate. It started as a colonial technique and now is perpetuated by chiefs for the same reason. (See paragraph [79] of the Sherman Labelle fatality inquiry report in the Appendix.)

In 1972 the community voted to have one chief. When Frank Kaquitts won, John Snow lied to the people and told them that three chiefs signed the treaty and if they didn't have three chiefs they would lose their treaty rights.

Greg Twoyoungmen, who has been a social activist for many years, is leading an effort to return to a single chief. It is his view that since there was a referendum by which the whole community made the change, the reversal by Snow was unlawful.

Right now, though, there are still three chiefs and 12 councillors, a separate administration for each of the divisions, and a fourth administration for the overall management. The salaries for the chiefs, councillors and administration staff total millions of dollars, but the schools are underfunded and the Stoney Medicine Lodge, which used to be a treatment centre for alcohol abuse, has been closed since 1996.

As my efforts to get to know people on the reserve progressed, the moccasin telegraph was apparently at work. One day in January of 1997 I received a call from Roy Pennoyer, the chief of the Stoney tribal police (another institution that has since been terminated). Roy suggested I might want to attend a training session on sentencing circles that was being put on in Edmonton by the RCMP's community policing division. He said it might help me understand Indigenous justice.

So I attended and it was a life-changing experience. The program was a facilitators training course in family group conferencing (now called community justice conferencing). It was presented by John M. McDonald and David Moore of Transformative Justice Australia, who had developed the process based on the Maori concept of the healing circle. The RCMP was sponsoring not only the training sessions but also the use of the process in conjunction with community policing.

As mentioned earlier, I was now some 50 years of age and had been a judge for almost two decades. And I was hearing the term "restorative justice" for the first time. The failure of the punitive justice system I worked in was becoming more and more apparent to me, but until I took this program I had no idea there was an alternative.

At the Aboriginal Justice Learning Network meeting in Calgary I also met Inspector Brad Holman. He told me the RCMP would put the family group conferencing training program on for any community that would provide enough people to participate. I arranged for it to be presented at Nakoda Lodge on the Stoney reserve and it was attended by more than 30 people – police officers, probation officers, victim services personnel, members of the Tsuu T'ina Nation/Stoney Corrections Society and a few Stoney elders.

It was at this program that I met Bert Wildman, one of the elders in attendance, who was also Marjorie Powderface's father.

Apparently I was having a far greater impact on the Stoney community than I realized. I was the white judge who had taken an interest in the community and declared my intention to deal with offenders in a culturally sensitive manner. I still did not fully understand the deep scars that had been left by Canadian colonialism, but I saw the poverty and social dysfunction that were pushing such a disproportionate number of these people into my courtroom every day, and I felt an obligation to do something about it.

When I asked my chief judge to support me in putting on the community justice conferencing training program, he told me it was inappropriate for me to be involved in the presentation of such a program. His view was that it would compromise my judicial independence to be involved in a program presented by the RCMP. I didn't agree with him and I went ahead with the program, but this was the beginning of a long conflict with the administration of my court.

❖ 4 ❖

RESTORATIVE JUSTICE

For me, justice on the Stoney Indian Reserve would be every
child having a safe, quiet place to sleep at night.
— Comment by author
to former Stoney Chief Ernest Wesley

I embraced the concepts I had learned at the community justice conferencing training session and I was anxious to use them.

"The community" is defined very simply as "those who did it and those who had it done to them." This encompasses anyone affected by the offence, and includes people related to the offender.

The results of these community justice circles were amazing. In my view they demonstrated the power of conversation and forgiveness.

A few stand out in my memory. One of them, with about a hundred people in the room, was also one of the most intimidating events of my career.

Lazarus Wesley and his wife, Lily Wesley, both Stoney elders, were at the Chiniki restaurant at Morley after an emotional funeral. The deceased had been murdered. One of their granddaughters became engaged in a fight with one of the cooks at the restaurant. She and the cook had a child together and there was a dispute about child support. The police were called. They arrested the granddaughter. What they saw was a woman causing a disturbance in a public place, harassing a man at his place of employment. Lazarus was probably in his late 70s at the time, but when he saw the police taking his granddaughter he interfered. There was a scuffle between the officer and the elder in the parking lot. Lily came to the aid of her husband and attempted to hit the officer with her cane. The parking lot was icy. She slipped and fell, sustaining some minor injuries. The police took both of them into custody and charged Lazarus with assaulting a police officer.

Lenny Wesley, one of the Wesleys' sons, was determined to sue the RCMP for the way they had treated his parents, and there would never be any co-operation between the reserve and the police. People were afraid of Lenny. Years earlier he had had a fight with a man and shot and killed him. He was found guilty of manslaughter and sentenced to a lengthy period of imprisonment. When he heard I was planning a circle to deal with this present situation, he told his parents not to attend. We couldn't have the circle without them, so with my usual disregard for protocol, I invited them to come to my house and talk about it.

My wife, Laura, made us lunch and we sat at the dining room table and had a very pleasant visit. Lazarus brought a picture of himself as an auxiliary peace officer. He was proud of his past service with the RCMP but angry about that rude young officer who had arrested him.

I encouraged him to come to the circle and see if we could reach a resolution of a matter that went beyond his own wounded pride, and he agreed.

The Cochrane detachment of the RCMP had been working at establishing a working relationship with the reserve and were very concerned about the overall effect of this unfortunate incident.

We convened the circle in the board room of the provincial building in Cochrane. There were far too many people to fit in a circle so I directed that only those who had been present at the restaurant would sit in the inner circle and everyone else would remain in the room but outside the circle. Lazarus sat on my left with Lily to his left and their family to their left. The police officers sat on my right. It must have been intimidating for them. They were almost the only non-Stoney people in the room and the atmosphere was somewhat tense. My biggest concern was controlling Lenny and his brother, Peter, who I was afraid might be very disruptive.

So I set out the procedure and said I only wanted the people in the inner circle to speak, and we began. Everyone talked about what happened and how they felt about it. The granddaughter talked about the difficulties with her child and the child's father. The grandparents talked about seeing their granddaughter taken into custody. The young police officers talked about the crowd they faced at the restaurant and trying to control what looked like an explosive situation. The officer who had the altercation with Lazarus apologized for his disrespect to the elder. Lazarus seemed impressed with his sincerity.

Then the amazing thing happened. Lenny said he had something to say. With some trepidation I told him to go ahead and speak. He addressed the young police officers and he said that, having heard everyone speak, he was satisfied they had done the best they could in the circumstances. The police officers said they too had a better understanding of the situation and would withdraw the assault charge against Lazarus. With Lenny's blessing, everyone was satisfied.

If there had been a civil suit against the RCMP and a trial of the charge against Lazarus, the damage to the relationship between the reserve and the RCMP could have been devastating. Both situations were resolved by the power of conversation and communication.

One of the people who took the training course at Nakoda Lodge was Keith Kloster, the Cochrane probation officer. He suggested he use the process in a case where I had convicted a young man of a sexual assault. I had ordered a presentence report, and in the ordinary course Keith would have produced the report after conducting interviews with people he considered appropriate to give information about the accused. But he thought this was a great case to do a conference because both the young man and the young woman belonged to the same church, so there was a community connection he thought would contribute to a resolution. I agreed with him and told him to go ahead with it.

The case did not fit within the guidelines, because the offender had entered a plea of not guilty and had been convicted after a trial. He contended he had simply given the young woman a friendly pat on her posterior. She testified in a very embarrassed manner that she felt his fingers "in the middle." I had no doubt that this was an unwanted touching of a sexual nature and the offence was made out.

When Keith spoke to the young woman, she didn't want to participate. She had found giving testimony difficult and embarrassing, and didn't want to have anything more to do with it. Keith asked me if I would speak to her, and so I did. I'm sure my chief judge would have found this to be grounds for a misconduct hearing before the Judicial Council. A judge speaking to a witness out of court was a breach of protocol, but I was more interested in resolution than protocol. I told her she might find it very helpful to engage in this process and encouraged her to do so. She agreed.

The circle consisted of the victim, her mother, sister, brother-in-law and two of her friends, the offender, his common-law spouse and three of his friends, a police officer, Keith and another probation officer.

The day after the conference Keith came into my office. He seemed very pleased with the result. He commented that he "felt like a horse that had been rode hard and put away wet," but he said it was worth it.

Keith died of cancer on September 23, 2001.

Some time later I wrote a letter to the editor of the *Cochrane Eagle*, which they published under the headline "Town will miss Kloster, a peacemaker above all." I think I must have been somewhat inspired when I wrote it. This what I said:

> The town of Cochrane has suffered a great loss with the passing of Keith Kloster. I have lost a good friend and a steadfast ally in the fight for better justice for all.
>
> Keith was Cochrane's probation officer from May of 1995 until he fell ill with cancer last year.
>
> He embraced the concept of community justice because he saw a benefit to the whole community when those in conflict with the law are both made to answer to the community and given the opportunity to make amends for their wrongdoing.
>
> He was a certified facilitator for community justice forums and an enthusiastic proponent of this process which brings offenders and victims together to come to an agreement that will satisfy the victim and be one that the offender is willing to perform in order to repair the harm done by an offence. Keith worked in the founding of the Cochrane Youth Justice Committee and supported the work of the Cochrane Victim's Assistance Program.
>
> He went above and beyond the duties of his job as a probation officer and made a tremendous contribution to maintaining peace in his community.
>
> In the Sermon on the Mount, Jesus said: "Blessed are the peacemakers for they shall be called the children of God." Keith was a peacemaker. He truly deserves to be called one of the children of God.

The following are excerpts from Keith's report:

> The conference formally began at 6:45 pm and lasted until 9:15 pm. The conference format was followed, wherein: the

accused spoke first about the offence; the victim spoke about her reaction to the offence; the victim's supporters described their reactions; the accused's supporters described their reactions; Cpl. Johnson gave the police viewpoint. The accused then spoke after hearing the effects on all present. Then, starting with the victim, all were able to express what they wanted to come out of the conference, which was written up as an agreement.

When the accused spoke the second time he expressed a great deal of regret and remorse over the offence, as he realized the serious impact it had upon all involved. He indicated he saw a need for attending counselling and expressed the desire that he and his family attend counselling together. He said that he feared having contact with the victim since the offence occurred. The victim and her supporters were surprised by this comment and the victim appeared more at ease. Her fear seemed to diminish and her confidence restored by the end of the conference.

The victim and her supports freely volunteered their opinion that a jail term was not necessary.

As the facilitator I felt this was a very successful family group conference. I believe the victim now feels safer, feels less victimized and can now put the offence behind her. I believe the accused recognizes the need to deal with personal and family issues through a counsellor. He seems over the past six months to have made some positive changes in his life through obtaining steady employment, becoming involved in a common-law relationship where he has taken on co-responsibility for the care of a three-year-old boy. He seems prepared to take the necessary steps to avoid further conflict with the law. The victim expressed to the writer that she was pleased with her difficult decision to participate and felt a real sense of success. All involved reflected similar sentiments that something positive came out of this difficult experience and incident that had occurred.

In the ordinary course of sentencing an offender such as this, I might have assessed a substantial fine, perhaps $1,000, or even 30 days imprisonment. That would have done nothing to resolve the underlying dysfunction, or to give closure to the victim or the accused.

Under the current law, passed by the government of Stephen Harper, this accused would have faced a minimum of six months imprisonment. I believe this law is more criminal than the offence the accused committed. This is an example of why I resigned my appointment as a judge. I could not send people to prison when I was convinced that doing so, in many circumstances, was just wrong.

The young man in this case appears to have become a contributing member of his community. Six months in prison might well have ended his relationship and made it difficult or impossible to find employment. It could have done huge harm while costing taxpayers to maintain him in prison.

Prison is often just a lose/lose proposition.

None of those involved in this situation were Indigenous people, but the process based on the Indigenous healing circle worked amazingly well for them. It demonstrates the basic difference in perspective between the two approaches.

The non-Indigenous system condemns the wrongdoer and often destroys their life while doing society as a whole no good whatsoever.

The Indigenous way condemns the wrongful act, and in seeking to repair the damage done by it, often produces benefits for the victim, the community and the wrongdoer as well.

Both systems use shame, which is a disconnection from community. But the Indigenous method uses reintegrative shame, where the wrongdoer is temporarily disconnected but the restorative process helps him to reconnect. The non-Indigenous system uses stigmatizing shame, where a criminal record makes the disconnection permanent.

❖ 5 ❖

THE ORIGINS OF PROCESSES

I don't propose a separate system for Aboriginal people; I
propose the Indigenous justice for everyone
— The author

What we know about the culture of Indigenous people before Contact with Europeans is limited because they had no written records, and much of what was written post-1492 was written by Europeans who had a vested interest in discrediting the people they found here. The Europeans wanted the land and just took it, but they also wanted to justify what they did. It is more justifiable to take land from vicious savages than to take it from people who are gentle, peaceful and generous.

So, there are stories of Indian torture and massacres and taking scalps from each other and from innocent white settlers. Many non-Indigenous people have the impression that this is what the Indigenous people were doing before they received the benefit of good, white, Christian influence. In my view all of the negative information about the Indigenous people is suspect because of the bias of the European people who wrote about them.

A good example is found in *The Inconvenient Indian*. Thomas King tells of a plaque erected in the town of Almo, Idaho, that reads:

> Dedicated to the memory of those who lost their lives in a most horrible Indian massacre, 1861. Three hundred immigrants west bound. Only five escaped.
>
> — Erected by the S&D of Idaho Pioneers, 1938

He goes on to tell of the research of a University of Utah professor, Brigham Madsen, who could find no record of the incident in any of the newspapers or military reports of the day and concluded that it never happened.

Another example of the probable falsity of stories told about the Indigenous people is the work of Joseph Boyden. His novel *The Orenda* tells of terrible atrocities committed by the Haudenosaunee (Iroquois) against the Wyandot (Huron). I found the descriptions of violence to be excessive, and was somewhat relieved to learn that Boyden's claim to have Indigenous ancestry has been disputed. Even though the book is fiction it has the potential of having readers believe that the kind of cruelty described did in fact occur. Hopefully the doubts cast on his ancestry will create doubts about the historical accuracy of his story.

If there are true stories of atrocities committed by Indigenous people, I say we have to look at the time when they occurred. We should distinguish between the way they were before Contact and the way they became after being subjected to the cruel culture of the European newcomers.

As a child I watched American movies and thought of the Apaches as vicious, scalp-taking savages. In more recent years, as a result of efforts to understand the Indigenous people, I now believe that the practice of scalping started with the Spanish. The Apache may have learned it from them and done it in retaliation.

I have developed an increasing appreciation of the basic goodness of the Indigenous people, both from the people I came to know and from my study of history.

It is important to remember that when Europeans started coming here in the 1500s and 1600s, the Indigenous people had strong, well-organized societies that could have easily driven out the newcomers. Instead of that, they welcomed them and helped them settle.

When Columbus landed somewhere in the Bahamas in 1492, the Arawak people greeted him with gifts and food.

When Champlain lost half of his men in the ill-fated settlement at Île Sainte-Croix, the Mi'kmaq came in the spring and saved the remaining half by showing them the herbs that cured the scurvy that was killing them.

When boatloads of Europeans landed on the shores of what is now the United States, the inhabitants there showed them how to plant corn and helped them survive.

People who were accustomed to fighting with each other would be unlikely to greet strangers in this manner. I conclude that they were living in peace with each other and were generally peaceful people.

I suggest we even owe the gentle, peaceful nature of our country to the Indigenous people. In his book *A Fair Country*, John Ralston Saul presents a good argument that Canada has a much gentler society than our neighbour to the south because we have experienced a much greater influence by the Indigenous people. Canada was initially settled by explorers and traders who intermarried with Indigenous women, creating a large Metis population. The United States, on the other hand, was settled by dissident religious groups who came as whole families and communities unto themselves and thus their interaction with the Indigenous people was much less than in Canada. One indicator of our more peaceful country is the murder rate, which is a fraction of what it is in the U.S.

Canada may well owe its existence as an independent nation to the Indigenous people and in particular Chief Tecumseh of the Shawnee.

In 1812 President James Madison persuaded an already bellicose Congress to declare war on England and its colonies and ordered his armies to march north and capture the colonies of Upper and Lower Canada. The 17 American states had a population of over seven million, while the population of Canada was barely 400,000. We really wouldn't have had a chance were it not for the intervention of Tecumseh, who led a federation of Indian Nations and entered the war as allies of England in order to stop American expansion into the Ohio Valley. It is said that 10,000 of his people died in fighting that war. They weren't all killed in battle; many of them died from diseases they caught from the other militants. But Tecumseh made a tremendous contribution to the defence of what is now Canada, and had he not, we might well have become part of the USA.

The big losers in the War of 1812 were the Indigenous people. In addition to the thousands who died in combat and from disease, the Ohio Valley was lost to the Americans and the unabated military expansion of American settlement continued into other Indigenous lands.

My efforts to learn about the Indigenous people have convinced me that before the coming of the Europeans the Indigenous people of the Americas were a much gentler people than the newcomers.

There are many examples of atrocities committed by the Europeans against the Indigenous people. To name a few:

In 1495 Columbus returned to the Bahamas with 17 ships and 1,200 men and enslaved the whole Arawak nation. The natives were treated with such cruelty that they are now extinct.

The English in Newfoundland hunted the Beothuk to extinction.

Governor Cornwallis paid a bounty on Mi'kmaq scalps in Nova Scotia.

In Canada the Indigenous military support during the War of 1812 was soon forgotten. The expanding European population and the diminishing Indigenous numbers changed the balance of power, and a century and a half of colonialism followed.

England developed one of the most powerful empires in history. It did so in part through piracy and the slave trade.

The English judicial system has its origins in the time of William the Conqueror, who came to England in 1066. The system developed through centuries in which the only behaviour modification technique known was terrorism. They used brutal punishments and public executions to frighten people into obeying the law. One was "drawing and quartering" – hanging a man until he was half dead and then cutting open his abdomen while he was still alive so he would see his innards spilling out, then dismembering him. In the navy a sailor who struck an officer was "whipped through the fleet" – tied in a boat and whipped with a cat-o'-nine-tails as the boat was rowed amongst the ships to "deter" others from committing similar offences. Many died in the process.

I don't condemn the present-day English for the atrocities of their ancestors, but I do say we should take a long look at the culture of cruelty and savagery from whence our criminal justice system came and ask ourselves if such a system is really worth keeping.

Then we should look at the history and culture of the Indigenous people and all that we owe them, and give serious thought to using their system rather than our own.

❖ 6 ❖

THE EVIL CORNWALLIS

The evil that men do lives after them;
The good is oft interred with their bones.
— William Shakespeare, *Julius Caesar*

My proposition is that the dominant Canadian society should scrap its criminal justice system and replace it with the gentler, and more effective, process used by the Indigenous people.

In the previous chapter I supported this proposition by referring to the goodness of the Indigenous people at the time of Contact and the evil of the Europeans, from whom our current system came.

My point is that the system came from a culture of cruelty and evil and still contains much cruelty and evil, and that we should be working at eliminating those.

I believe the criminal justice system is wrong in condemning wrongdoers when it should be focusing on the wrongdoing. When someone does something wrong, our system wants to totally destroy them, along with all of the good they may have done.

In January of 2018, as I was working on the manuscript of this book, the City of Halifax removed the statue of Edward Cornwallis from its granite pedestal on Hollis Street. This seems to have been done largely out of fear. The statue was a source of controversy and demonstrations by those for and against removing it.

While I do not think the evil of Cornwallis can be overstated, I disagree with the removal of the statue.

His Scalping Proclamation of 1749, which some say resulted in mercenaries bringing in baskets full of Mi'kmaq scalps, was not the only evil thing he did. He was also part of the murder of some 2,000 Scots after the Battle of Culloden in 1746, in what was called the Pacification of the Highlands.

In the battle of Culloden, Bonnie Prince Charlie was defeated by the English army under the Duke of Cumberland. When the battle was clearly lost and Bonnie Prince Charlie had fled from the field, Cumberland ordered the "pacifying" of the Western Highlands. This meant the execution of the surviving Scots. As many as 2,000 were killed after the battle was over, by forces under the command of Cornwallis along with James Wolfe, who later led the English army that defeated the French on the Plains of Abraham. They boarded up suspected Jacobite families in their homes and set them on fire, and looted the countryside.

With this background, Cornwallis was appointed Governor of Nova Scotia. Part of his mission was to found a settlement at the site of present-day Halifax, which he did. But he did it in Mi'kmaq territory, "without consultation." He just considered the Mi'kmaq a problem. He was typical of the imperialist attitude of his time. He was a white supremacist and he committed genocide in the advancement of his own ambitions.

But should his statue be removed? It is my view that if we are truly interested in truth and reconciliation, we should not hide the truth. The truth is that this evil man is a part of our history. There is nothing wrong with rewriting history, especially when the original version is distorted. I suggest the better way to deal with this is to admit the truth by leaving the statue and doing something to tell the rest of the story. Perhaps a statue to commemorate the Mi'kmaq genocide as well, with a plaque to the effect of:

This statue of Governor Cornwallis was erected at a time when the atrocities of Canadian colonialism were not acknowledged and instead the imperialism of the past was honoured. Today we recognize that this man, though credited with founding the City of Halifax, took the land from its lawful owners the Mi'kmaq people and committed genocide in so doing.

Daniel Paul, author of *We Were Not the Savages*, has suggested that a statue honouring Donald Marshall should replace that of Cornwallis. Perhaps they could stand together so that the whole truth is on display.

If we discard the statue of Cornwallis and rename the park and schools, what about Sir John A. Macdonald? Our first prime minister made a huge contribution to creating the confederation that is now Canada and inspired the construction of the railway that brought about the expansion of the nation from sea to sea. The good the man did can hardly be overstated, but neither can the evil. His policies of assimilating the Indigenous people into the dominant society were clearly genocidal and the damage they have done lives on. So are we going to take his name off of every school, take down every statue and pretend he just didn't exist? I doubt this will happen, but if we really want to have truth and reconciliation, I would suggest that putting a plaque on every school and statue telling the truth about him and apologizing to the Indigenous people would be a step in the right direction.

I say that the most important element of reconciliation is respect. I don't believe the dominant society shows respect to the Indigenous people by hiding the past. I believe it shows respect by admitting the past and changing its present-day attitude.

❖ 7 ❖

MILTON BORN WITH A TOOTH

The panel said the project was "not acceptable" and rec-
ommended that the dam be decommissioned.
— Jack Glenn, *Once Upon an Oldman*

I believe that one of the worst examples of disrespect to the Indigenous people of Alberta was the construction of the Oldman River dam by the provincial government and the imprisonment of Milton Born With a Tooth for his part in opposing the project.

His case was a big part of the change in my thinking about the justice system and the plight of the Indigenous people generally.

Milton was one of the leaders of the Lonefighters, a group of Piikani Indigenous people who opposed the construction of the dam. The Piikani did not necessarily want to prevent the project altogether, but they were concerned about potential damage to the environment and to archeological sites that were of vital importance to their spiritual and cultural heritage. They actually favoured a site on their reserve and made a proposal to the Alberta government to that effect.

The government wanted to build the dam to make more water available to the Lethbridge Northern Irrigation District. Political considerations far outweighed environmental concerns. There was virtually no regard for the Piikani and their spiritual and cultural interest in the area to be affected.

I am embarrassed to admit that at the time this struggle was happening I did not pay much attention to it. This was occurring before my "conversion on the road to Morley," as it were. I was still living in Calgary and assigned to the Provincial Court there. The news of the events on the Oldman River was not of particular interest to me, but the controversy surrounding the construction of the dam and the efforts by the Lonefighters were very much a subject of conversation in the judges' lounge. When Milton was charged and the legal proceeding against him went on for several years, I recall some of my fellow judges referring to him as Milton Born-With-a-Legal-Aid-Certificate. I was a little uncomfortable about the disparaging comments but didn't say anything.

I suppose that if I had been asked for my opinion at that time I would have said I thought Milton was just a crazy Indian and a troublemaker. I trusted that the government of Alberta knew what it was doing, and that if they were going to build this dam, it must be the right thing to do.

So none of this meant much to me until I was transferred to Canmore, with Cochrane added to the Canmore circuit, and I started my quest to get to know the Stoney Nakoda people. In the course of my new program of learning, which included Indigenous culture generally, I attended a cultural camp hosted by Reg Crowshoe, a Piikani elder. We camped in teepees on the plain below the Head-Smashed-In Buffalo Jump. The conference sessions were held in a large double teepee – something I had never seen before. The frames of two teepees were intermeshed and the canvases stretched around both so that the two made one in the form of a figure 8. Here, with a fire burning in the middle of one tent, there were presentations by elders. Mrs. Potts talked at some length about the devastation of the flood and the tremendous loss of their spiritual and cultural heritage. I was confused by her reference to "the flood" and I asked her what flood she was speaking of. She looked at me like I was from a different planet and she said with tremendous emotion: "When they built the dam!" Then she recovered her composure and she said: "Oh, I forgot, you're from the Stoneys."

Her comment was greeted by laughter by most of those present. I have been told by members of the Blackfoot Nations that the Stoney are often the butt of their jokes, much as we in Alberta would make "Newfies" the butt of ours. So once Mrs. Potts had realized that I was from the Stoneys, she seemed much more patient with my ignorance.

As has happened to me a number of times in my ongoing education, I realized the reality of something that had only been newspaper information to me before. Here was a woman who, years after the dam had been built, was still lamenting the loss she experienced as a result of "the flood."

So I wanted to overcome my ignorance about the dam. I read *Once Upon an Oldman*, by Jack Glenn, which I found very informative. (At the time of Glenn's writing, the Piikani were called "Peigan" and this is the word I will use when quoting him.)

In his preface Glenn says:

> My purposes in researching and writing this book were to provide a clear and coherent account of the Oldman controversy, to show how it revealed the disparities between what our governments say about the environment and Indian people and how they act towards them, and to illustrate the impotence of special interest groups in effecting changes that are contrary to the received wisdom.

The facts he sets out are an indictment of the conduct of the Conservative governments of Peter Lougheed and Don Getty, as well as the work of Ralph Klein when he was the environment minister. In his introduction Glenn gives a concise statement of the Indigenous/non-Indigenous conflict:

> Over the years, the Oldman river and the valley through which it flows have meant different things to different people. For the Peigan tribe of the Blackfoot Indian Nation, they

are a birthright and a homeland, an ancestral burial ground, a source of spiritual strength, and the thread that binds the Native people with the natural environment. They also offer the potential for economic development on the Peigan reserve that could contribute to the well-being of its impoverished residents.

For southern Alberta's farming community, the Oldman is the prime source of water for the irrigation that is the basis for its existence in this perennially water-short area. ...

Glenn sets out the political history. In 1971 the Conservatives under Peter Lougheed won the provincial election, but they didn't get a single seat in the "irrigation belt," the 12 provincial constituencies in southern Alberta which are dependent on irrigation. Before the next election, the Conservatives promised to make irrigation a priority, and in the 1975 race they took nine of the 12 seats.

The pro-irrigation bias of the government was demonstrated by a number of things. One was the termination of the Environment Conservation Authority, which had been created by the Social Credit government in 1970. In 1974 the Authority had opposed a dam on the Paddle River and in 1977 opposed one on the Red Deer River. So in 1977 the agency was terminated and replaced by the Environmental Council of Alberta, which was constituted differently. In place of a permanent panel, panellists were appointed for each hearing.

To counter rumours that the panel members would be selected on the basis of their pro-dam sentiments, the government invited eighteen different groups to nominate candidates for the three panel positions, but tipped its hand by indicating it was looking for panellists with some knowledge of farming, water storage, and community interest in irrigation. Knowledge of the environment or Indians were not prerequisites.

In spite of the fact that the new panel was expected to be more favourable to the government position, it released a report in August 1979 which said "an on stream dam is not required at this time, nor in the foreseeable future." Its recommendation was that there would be sufficient water storage in a number of off-stream reservoirs, making a dam unnecessary.

In spite of these recommendations, just a year later, in August 1980, the government announced plans to build a dam on the Oldman River.

There were three proposed sites. One, at Fort Macleod, was the most environmentally friendly but was too low to allow water to flow to the irrigation system, and pumping would be an untenable ongoing expense. The next was at Brocket, on the Piikani reserve, and the worst was at the confluence of the Oldman, Castle and Crowsnest rivers – the Three Rivers site.

Before a dam at either Brocket or Three Rivers could be of use, the headworks of the irrigation system, which were located on the reserve, had to be upgraded, but there was a dispute about this. In 1922 the Lethbridge Northern Irrigation District had purchased a 250-acre right-of-way to build the water diversion, but the Piikani took the position that the right-of-way was granted without their consent. So in 1978 they blockaded the area. In order to end the blockade the province promised to enter into negotiations for the ongoing use of the headworks. When the promised negotiations did not occur the Piikani filed an application in the Alberta Court of Queen's Bench for a declaration that the 1922 transfer was invalid. The province then entered negotiation in 1979.

A negotiated settlement of the headworks dispute was reached in April 1981, and the Piikani offered to enter into talks to build the dam at Brocket. They were awaiting the government's response when, on August 9, 1984, Premier Lougheed announced that construction of the dam would begin in 1986 at the Three Rivers site.

This site was opposed by the Piikani, environmentalists and sport fishermen represented by the Alberta Fish and Game Association, Alberta Wilderness Association, Canadian Nature Federation, Canadian Parks and Wilderness Society, Federation of Alberta Naturalists, Trout Unlimited and the 16 farming families that would be displaced by the dam and forced out of their homes.

The Three Rivers site was more costly and would do greater damage to the environment and archeological sites, but Alberta apparently did not want to work in co-operation with the Piikani Nation.

The environmental damage would include not only destruction of the last large stocks of bull trout in southern Alberta, but also loss of riparian poplar forests downstream from the dam and all the biodiversity they contained.

The province promised that archaeological damage would be mitigated by the recovery of artifacts. and government retained Dr. Brian Reeves to do the study for the mitigation project. Reeves apparently came to the opinion that the damage could not be properly mitigated, and in 1987 he recommended that the site be designated a provincial historical resource and that the Oldman River dam should not be constructed.

As to the concerns of the Piikani, Glenn wrote the following:

> Although the preponderance of the archaeological finds inventoried at the site – teepee rings, buffalo drive sites, campsites – were of Indian origin, there was no suggestion that the various Blackfoot bands, whose ancestors' lifestyles and very existence were recorded by the finds, would be consulted on the mitigation plan.
>
> ... Both the Alberta Historical Resources Act and the Archaeological Survey of Alberta exhibit strange attitudes towards the interest of Native peoples in archaeological

resources located within the areas traditionally occupied by their ancestors. The Act claims all artifacts found in Alberta as the property of the Crown. It makes no allowance whatever for consultation with Indian people on the interpretation of sites or artifacts; on their significance to Indian history, culture or religion; or on the handling or management of any archaeological materials found in areas of traditional Indian occupation....

In the case of the Oldman River dam, the Peigan were not consulted on the interpretation or disposition of the materials discovered during the impact study or on the design and implementation of the mitigation program. Although consultation with residents was a requirement in the inventory and assessment of historical resources, consultation with Indian people was not included in the terms of reference for the archaeological resources.

In 1986 construction began with the excavation of diversion tunnels. When the project required work in the river, Alberta Environment issued itself a licence under the Water Resources Act (August 1987). The Act required that anyone applying to build a dam had to give public notice of the application. Alberta Environment did not do this.

Those opposed to the dam formed a society called the Friends of the Oldman River (FOR).

On September 4, 1987, FOR sued for an injunction to stop construction on the dam. There had been no public notice of the application to build it and the province had failed to obtain the permission of the Municipal District of Pincher Creek, the authority responsible for roads that would be inundated, and failed to refer the application to the Energy Resources Conservation Board (ERCB), all of which were measures required by the Water Resources Act.

In December of 1987 the licence was quashed by Justice Kenneth Moore, because of the failure to obtain the required clearances from the ERCB and the M.D. of Pincher Creek. The province appealed the order and continued with construction.

In February 1988 the province simply reissued the licence and abandoned the appeal. FOR challenged the second licence, but by then the province had corrected some of its original errors and there had been so much publicity attached to it that the lack of public notice was not fatal. This meant that groups with an interest in the construction of the dam were not given a chance to be heard.

On August 2, 1988, Dr. Martha Kostuch, an environmental activist and one of the founders of FOR, laid charges against the environment minister as well as the project manager and two of the construction companies, for destroying fish habitat contrary to the federal Fisheries Act. She thought the federal Department of Justice would prosecute the case, but the Alberta Attorney General took it over instead and stayed the charges for insufficient evidence.

(A private citizen who has grounds can in fact lay a charge against any other citizen and prosecute the charge. However, a Crown prosecutor may at any time take control of such a prosecution. In this and several other matters where FOR sought to prosecute government officials and employees who appeared to be committing unlawful acts, the provincial government intervened, took control of the charges and entered a stay of proceedings.)

On March 10, 1987, Alberta applied to Transport Canada for approval under the Navigable Waters Protection Act to construct the dam. The Act required an environmental assessment prior to approval. On September 18, 1987, the federal Minister of Transport issued the approval without requiring the environmental assessment.

In the meantime the Southern Alberta Environmental Group had written to the federal Minister of Fisheries and Oceans asking for an environmental impact assessment of the dam. The minister simply said that problems were being addressed and he was not disposed to intervene.

In December 1987 FOR wrote to the federal Minister of Environment requesting that the Oldman dam be subjected to an Environmental Assessment Review Process Guidelines Order (EARPGO). The minister replied that to intervene would be inappropriate.

The Piikani asked Indian Affairs to apply an EARPGO. In March 1989, the minister said he would refer the matter to the environment minister.

In April 1989 FOR applied in Federal Court to quash the approval under the Navigable Waters Protection Act, on the ground that it had been granted without the environmental impact assessment.

Prior to making the application, FOR had met with Ralph Klein, the newly appointed minister of the environment. Klein had been expected to be supportive of the environmental issues but he told FOR that even if the Federal Court ruled in favour of their application, Alberta would not stop work on the dam.

For's Federal Court application was unsuccessful and they appealed to the Federal Court of Appeal. On March 13, 1990, the Federal Court of Appeal quashed the Navigable Waters Protection Act approval and ordered the Ministry of Transport and Ministry of Fisheries and Oceans to comply with the EARPGO.

Alberta appealed this decision to the Supreme Court of Canada and kept working on the dam. It justified the continued work on grounds that leaving the dam partially completed created a safety issue. The federal government was also bound by the ruling of the Federal Court of Appeal and should have taken steps to enforce the guidelines order, but it did not.

It was also incumbent upon the federal Minister of Environment to proceed with the environmental assessment, but the minister was not acting. For then took out a notice of motion to compel the minister to proceed. On November 16, 1991, a few days before the application was to be heard, the minister's office announced that a review panel had been appointed. Alberta tried to stop the review, pending their appeal to the Supreme Court of Canada, but the application was unsuccessful and the review went ahead while the Supreme Court action was in course.

The panel held hearings in November 1991 in which they considered over 100 presentations and 137 written submissions.

In January 1992 the Supreme Court upheld the Federal Court ruling that obliged the government to apply the EARPGO to the dam project. This ruling confirmed the work of the panel, which was in the process of assimilating all the material it had received and preparing its report.

Glenn gives the following summary of the panel's report:

> In early May 1992, the panel submitted its report and recommendations to the federal ministers. The panel said the project was "not acceptable" and recommended that the dam be decommissioned. It concluded the environmental impacts of the project would be severe. The loss of fishery resources would be significant, greatly outweighing any potential gains from the project, and there was no certainty, in the panel's estimation, that the loss of the riparian cottonwood ecosystems downstream from the dam could be avoided. Because of the inadequacy of Alberta's work, the panel had been unable to determine the full extent of the project's consequences for wildlife and biological diversity. While noting that Alberta Culture had implemented an "ambitious" program to salvage archaeological and historical artifacts from the reservoir area, the panel observed that "the scientific and cultural value of

these artifacts is diminished when the artifacts are taken out of context." Coming down firmly on the side of the government's original consulting archaeologist, Dr. Brian Reeves, the panel concluded that "the existence of a record of the unique cultural achievement of the bison hunters, in situ, is important provincially, nationally and internationally. The irreversible loss of an area which contains so much historic and prehistoric information is a significant cost of the project."

The panel believed that the project had, and would continue to have, significant adverse social and cultural consequences for the Peigan. It found that the Peigan were not sufficiently involved in decisions about the project, one outstanding example of which was that no Native people were interviewed during the course of the historic sites studies. The panel called this oversight "inexcusable" because it "overlooks a very important source of local information." It found that cottonwoods, fish, game and willows – resources important to Peigan culture – would be affected by the project, that mercury contamination of fish downstream from the dam would be a threat to the health of the Peigan, and that sites within the reservoir area with cultural and spiritual value to the Peigan would be flooded.

So, with this background information (for which I now have a much better appreciation than I did in the 1990s) I will briefly describe the involvement of Milton Born With a Tooth.

On August 3, 1990, he and a group of Piikani called the Lonefighters rented a bulldozer and began an attempt to breach the dike that channelled water into the irrigation district's headworks. Their intention was to divert the river into a dry channel. Work was slow due to mechanical difficulties and the bulldozer getting mired in the soft earth, but on August 28 they breached the dike, causing a minimal amount of flow from the river into the dry channel.

On August 29 Alberta obtained an injunction forbidding anyone from preventing water from entering the weir intake, and the following morning a force of 20 to 50 RCMP officers attended to serve the injunction.

There was mixed support for the Lonefighters on the Piikanii tribal council, but Chief Leonard Bastien was sympathetic to them. He met with the RCMP commissioner and asked for an agreement that the RCMP would not come on the reserve in large numbers and would give him two days notice of any action they might take.

Alberta Environment was anxious to repair the damage to the dike and sent a work crew onto the reserve with an armed RCMP escort on September 7.

In spite of an undertaking the RCMP had given Chief Bastien, they came without giving the notice and with a force of almost 90 men – a 16-member emergency response team (to infiltrate the camp the night before to report on status), a 36-member escort for Alberta Environment work crews, a 30-member tactical troop to control any demonstrators, and several female officers. The emergency response team had entered the night before in camouflage uniforms and with automatic weapons in order to assess the situation and do a status report.

In the confrontational circumstances of the armed intrusion, Milton Born With a Tooth fired two shots. He says he fired them in the air; the RCMP say he fired at them. He was subsequently arrested, charged with weapons offences, denied bail and spent three months in custody awaiting trial. His first trial was before Justice Laurie Maclean. He was convicted by an all-white jury, and on March 25, 1991, he was sentenced to 18 months in prison. This first conviction was set aside on appeal due to the conduct of the judge, who demonstrated serious racial bias throughout the trial and was later the subject of a Judicial Council hearing in relation to that. The hearing resulted in an apology by Maclean and no further action was taken against him.

Milton Born With a Tooth was retried in February of 1994. He was again convicted, although the trial was much more respectful of Indigenous tradition. On September 9, 1994, he was sentenced to 16 months.

To summarize the conduct of the Alberta government:

1. They don't like the advice they are getting on dam construction from the Environmental Conservation Authority, so they reconstitute the Authority under a different name.
2. When the newly reconstituted panel also recommends against dam construction they ignore the recommendations.
3. When they need a permit, they issue it to themselves without complying with the requirements of their own legislation.
4. When the permit is quashed, they appeal the order and continue building.
5. They abandon the appeal and again issue a permit without giving public notice, which results in interested parties not being given an opportunity to be heard.
6. When their own archaeological consultant, Dr. Brian Reeves, says the dam should not be built, they discredit him.
7. When the Federal Court of Appeal confirms that the dam requires an environmental impact assessment, they appeal the judgment and keep on building.
8. On at least three occasions when FOR lays a private information in relation to illegal proceeding in the construction, the provincial Attorney General intervenes and stays the proceedings.
9. They build on the site which will cost more and do more environmental and archaeological damage, because they will not work in co-operation with the Piikani or include them in a joint project.
10. They go onto the Piikanii reserve, arguably the sovereign territory of Milton's people, in violation of their undertaking and in force.

In these circumstances, when a force of armed RCMP enter the reserve in breach of their own undertaking to give notice, Milton Born With a Tooth fires a rifle a couple of times and he is arrested, charged and imprisoned.

I see this as a horrid example of the justice system being used as an instrument of the oppression of Indigenous people.

Milton Born With a Tooth died at Calgary on May 18, 2019. His obituary described him as "a lifelong protector of the Blackfoot way of life and the lands and waters of the earth."

❖ 8 ❖

· THE RIGHT THING

*European justice systems are basically systems of terror-
ism, designed to frighten people into obeying the law.*
—The author

In my changing thinking, one of the most powerful concepts I discovered was the difference in focus between Eurocentric justice and Indigenous justice.

Our justice system focuses on people doing the wrong thing. It seems to be founded on the premise that people are basically evil. For this reason, they must be "deterred" from wrongdoing. The etymology of the word is the Latin *terrere*, to frighten. It has the same root as the English word "terror." European justice systems are basically systems of terrorism, designed to frighten people into obeying the law.

This philosophy has its roots in the days when kings ruled by divine right and the ordinary people were considered to be lesser human beings. The nobility owned their serfs, who weren't their equals and weren't deserving of respect.

In this day and age of our free and democratic society, we at least pay lip service to the concept that all men and women are equal. So why do we keep a system that has its roots in an age when the concept of equality was not even dreamed of? We say the Magna Carta was the beginning of democracy and the idea of trial by one's peers, but the peers were the very small group at the top of the social ladder, who considered ordinary people as their property.

The Indigenous systems are founded on the premise that people are basically good and wrongdoing is the aberration. So instead of dealing with the whole population as potential wrong-doers, they see the wrongdoers as the anomaly, as ordinary people who make mistakes, either from sickness or ignorance.

One of the interesting exercises in the restorative justice training program mentioned earlier was to discuss the reasons why people do the "right" thing. The consensus was that the main reason is respect: self-respect, respect for others, respect for everything in Creation.

The real problem in the Milton Born With a Tooth situation was that the government of Alberta showed a complete lack of respect. They showed none for the environment or the history that was being destroyed, none for the laws governing the construction of dams, and none for the people affected by the resulting "flood." The politicians who were in power wanted to stay in power, and they would do whatever was expedient to get the votes that would keep them there.

All Milton wanted was respect. Respect for the environment, for the historical, cultural and spiritual importance of the Three Rivers valley, and respect for his people and for himself.

My father used to quote Sir Wilfrid Laurier, who, in 1885 said of Louis Riel: "Had I been born on the banks of the Saskatchewan, I would myself have shouldered a musket...."

I admire what Milton did. It embarrasses me that the government of my province acted the way they did, and that my justice system, of which I was once so proud, was the instrument of his oppression.

I of course feel the same way about Louis Riel. If I had been in his situation I only hope that I too would have had the courage to shoulder a rifle against the imperialist crimes committed by the governments of Canada and Alberta.

❖ 9 ❖

RESPECT

Men are respectable only as they respect.
— Ralph Waldo Emerson

If we expect Indigenous people to respect the non-Indigenous justice system, the system has to do a better job of showing respect for them.

In October 2017 I spoke at a justice conference presented by the Institute for the Advancement of Aboriginal Women in Edmonton.

The reason for the conference was that there had been three cases that were of concern to the IAAW because of egregious disrespect shown to Indigenous women during the respective trials.

In *R. v. Wagar*, an Indigenous woman had complained of a rape. In the course of the trial the judge, Robin Camp, had made several inappropriate comments that disclosed a stereotypical attitude against women, the worst remark being "why didn't you just keep your knees together?" The original acquittal was set aside on appeal and a new trial ordered. The judge was the subject of a complaint to the Judicial Council. When the council recommended his removal he resigned his judicial appointment. In the new trial, heard by Judge Jerry LeGrandeur, the accused was again acquitted, because of inconsistencies in the complainant's evidence.

Judge LeGrandeur is a senior jurist and was assistant chief judge for the southern region of Alberta. He is well known for his fairness and I am confident he would have decided the retrial without any extraneous considerations. So Judge Camp seems to have been right in his final verdict, but the fact that he lost his job over his disrespectful comments reinforces the need to show respect, no matter what else you might think of a person.

In the case of *R. v. Blanchard*, another Indigenous complainant in a rape case also suffered from serious disrespect. In the course of the witness's testimony at a preliminary hearing the Crown prosecutor asked that she be held in custody because there was a fear she would not return to complete her testimony. She was held for five days. She was transported to the holding facility in the same van as the accused and required to testify while in shackles. The accused was an exceptionally violent man who had spent 34 years in penitentiaries, 18 of them for the manslaughter of a fellow prisoner whom he beat to death with an iron bar.

The case caused public indignation over the treatment of the witness, and the Alberta justice minister at the time, Kathleen Ganley, announced the matter would be investigated. She was quoted as saying, "One of the questions that keeps me up at night is whether it would have been the case that if this woman was Caucasian and housed and not addicted, this would have happened to her."

An independent review released in February 2018 stated that there was a complete breakdown of legal protections, but the investigator, Roberta Campbell, did not believe that anyone deliberately engaged in racist or discriminatory actions toward the victim. Evidently the shackling of incarcerated victims is common in the Edmonton jurisdiction. Even though physical restraints are only to be used when necessary, this policy is often not followed in practice. While the investigator found there was no racist or deliberately discriminatory action against the victim, she did recommend that all parties be provided with cultural competency training specifically concerning Indigenous victims and witnesses.

I have mixed feelings about the statement that there was no racist or discriminatory action. Like most Canadians, I like to think there is very little racism in Canada, and I am concerned that the investigator may have shared this predisposition. The fact is that many Indigenous people are the victims of racism, and our denial of its existence is one of the biggest obstacles to overcoming it.

The other aspect of this, which I have mentioned before, is that there is a bias against unkempt street people, and because of the history of the treatment of Indigenous people in Canada, they are overrepresented amongst the unkempt street people, just as they are in prisons and child welfare. So if one is biased against street people, it may be hard to distinguish that from a bias against Indigenous people.

An interesting footnote to this case is that Blanchard, after he was convicted, applied for a stay of his convictions and of a pending dangerous offender application against him, because his Charter rights had been violated. He complained of abuse by other prisoners and correctional programs officers; severely limited physical recreational opportunities and mental stimulation in administrative segregation; inadequate food and lack of appropriate utensils; insufficient medical services; and allegations of abuse by other inmates which involved human waste.

Justice Eric Macklin held that Blanchard's Charter rights to life, liberty and security of the person and to be free from cruel and unusual treatment or punishment were violated by this treatment, which was "grossly disproportionate and offensive to societal notions of fair play and decency."

While Justice Macklin agreed that Charter rights were violated, he declined to grant the remedy requested, on the basis that protection of the public outweighed the accused's right to a remedy. However, his finding that there were Charter violations is a confirmation that even persons serving time for the most egregious of crimes are entitled to respect.

Blanchard was subsequently designated a dangerous offender, which will result in his being reincarcerated indefinitely.

In the third case of concern to the IAAW, *R. v. Barton*, the charge was the first-degree murder of Cindy Gladue, an Indigenous woman who died after sexual activity with the accused that caused fatal hemorrhaging from an injury to her uterus. The accused maintained that the injury was sustained accidentally in consensual rough sex in which he inserted his hand into her vagina. Crown expert witnesses said the injury was consistent with the use of a sharp object, but no such object was found.

The accused was acquitted by a jury after a trial in which both the prosecutor and the defence lawyer referred to the deceased as "the prostitute" and "the native woman," and evidence of her prior sexual conduct was admitted without the proper legal steps. For these reasons the jury verdict of not guilty to both the charge of first degree murder and the included offence of manslaughter was set aside.

The case may actually improve and clarify the law in relation to sexual assault and the issue of consent. The Court of Appeal wrote a very strong judgment setting out the errors and outlining what should have been done. However, the most egregious aspect of the case was that the deceased woman's preserved pelvis was entered into evidence at the trial. That disrespect shown to Ms. Gladue's dignity during the trial process outraged women across Canada.

I suggest that it is unimaginable that the body parts of a "respectable" white woman would ever be admitted in evidence at a trial. I put the word respectable in quotations because it displays an attitude of the dominant white society. They would have too much respect for a white woman but they have no respect for an Indigenous woman.

In *The Inconvenient Indian* Thomas King says:

> ... as I argue in the book, when we look at Native/non-Native relations, there is no great difference between the past and the present. While we have dispensed with guns and bugles, and while North America's sense of its own superiority is better hidden, its disdain muted, 21st century attitudes towards Native people are remarkably similar to those of the previous centuries.

The big problem is that the dominant society does not show very much respect for the Indigenous people.

If the reason people do the right thing is respect, I suggest that taking away their respect contributes to wrongdoing.

I suggest further that a significant factor in the overrepresentation of Indigenous people in the prison system is that they have been treated with such disrespect by the Canadian state that many lack the self-respect that would have them doing the right things. Canadian colonialism told the Indigenous people that their languages shouldn't be spoken, that they could be charged criminally for their spiritual practices and that they weren't fit to raise their own children. How much more disrespect can a people be shown?

❖ 10 ❖

PARADIGM CHANGE

In order to change an existing paradigm you do not struggle to try and change the problematic model. You create a new model and make the old one obsolete.
— R. Buckminster Fuller

Probably my greatest claim to fame is that I changed my mind. The change of mind I'm talking about goes a little further than saying I'm going to have chocolate ice cream and then deciding I'm going to have vanilla instead. I changed the way I think about Indigenous people and about the justice system. I experienced a "paradigm change."

The reason why the Institute for the Advancement of Aboriginal Women asked me to speak at their justice conference was that they want change and I am an advocate for change.

I based my remarks to them on a book review I wrote for the *Alberta Law Review* a number of years ago. The book was *Ghost Dancing with Colonialism*, in which author Grace Woo examines 65 Supreme Court cases and rates them as to their colonial or postcolonial quality.

She points out the basic lack of objectivity on the court. The tribunal was created without input from the Aboriginal people. There are no Aboriginal members on the court. Laws which the court interprets and applies were passed without Aboriginal input, and in many cases at a time when Aboriginal people were not even considered persons.

Woo's basic message is that the way we thought in the past

made the prior treatment of Indigenous people seem okay. Today we acknowledge that this manner of treatment is not appropriate, but further changes in our thinking are required in order for the practice to correspond to the talk.

We have to change the way we think. (Einstein would agree.)

We have to change our paradigm.

Woo has a whole chapter on "paradigm." This is a word that has always given me difficulty, and when I was working on the book review in Taiwan, my son, Sean, explained it this way. A paradigm is the box of ideas from which we assess everything around us. There are accepted ideas that go in the box and there are rejected ideas that do not. The understanding of any issue is dependent on what is in the box. When issues arise that cannot be understood by what is in the box we refer to them as anomalies. When the anomalies persist, we are required to change the paradigm.

Paradigm change is a slow and difficult process. Before 1930 the Canadian paradigm did not include the idea that a woman was a person. A man in 1929 could say that all persons in Canada have the right to vote and he would be making a correct statement, even though women, Indians and Chinese people did not have that right. The notion that such individuals were persons was not in the 1929 box of ideas. In 1930, in *Edwards v. Canada*, the Judicial Committee of the Privy Council (U.K.) ruled that women are in fact persons. So, the post-1930 Canadian paradigm includes that idea.

Sometimes ideas are not even consciously formulated. There is a common belief that Indigenous people are just primitive, that they have had to come though 5,000 years of human development in only 500 years and they just need more time to catch up.

That pretty much described my own thinking at the time. It wasn't a consciously formulated idea, but if I had thought about it, I would probably have accepted the "primitive" theory.

I hope most people are beginning to see this as the racist, white supremacist attitude that it is. What it is really saying is that they are not okay the way they are but will be okay when they are just like us.

That is why Europeans looked down on the Indigenous people. To the Europeans, civilization was steel and gunpowder, money and the written word. When they saw a society that did not have these things they regarded it as primitive. The fact that the Indigenous society was so much more peaceful and gentle and that their own was cruel and savage did not occur to them.

"Colonialism" is another word that has given me difficulty. I used to think of it as describing the process of good, brave people going out into the wilderness to establish farms and communities. This was the accepted view back in the day when we thought of the Indigenous people as extinct or becoming extinct. The meaning of the word now, and as Grace Woo uses it, describes the process of one nation controlling another, taking away the freedom and right of self determination of the subject nation.

Colonialism in Canada was Indian treaties, Indian reserves, Indian agents, Indian residential schools and the Indian Act. The Truth and Reconciliation Commission referred to colonialism as cultural genocide. A former Chief Justice of the Supreme Court of Canada, Beverley McLachlin, also referred to it as cultural genocide. I say it was actual genocide. It involved the deaths of thousands of Indigenous people, including the children in the residential schools and many others who died of starvation and disease – the results of Canadian government action.

When Stephen Harper was prime minister, he said Canada had no history of colonialism. I think for him the word meant one country taking over another. He just didn't understand the process happening within the country itself – that the term referred to the dominant society totally controlling the Indigenous people in Canada.

Grace Woo asserts that even the granting of the vote to "Indians" in 1960 was in fact an act of colonialism. It simply told the Aboriginal peoples that they were citizens of Canada without asking them if they wanted to be citizens of Canada. The fact that they live in the geographic area covered by what is known as Canada does not deprive Indigenous people of the right to determine for themselves whether or not they will be citizens of Canada.

Woo sets out a number of historical facts that are crucial to our understanding of the right of self-determination of Aboriginal people. Section 35 of the Constitution Act, 1982, as well as the United Nations Declaration on the Rights of Indigenous Peoples, which Canada has now signed, have theoretically confirmed these rights, but the struggle to put them into practice continues. The first of these rights is the right of sovereignty, symbolized by the two-row wampum, representing the treaty between the Haudenosaunee Confederacy and the Europeans. The two purple rows on the background of white symbolize the separation of the nations. The Iroquois never agreed to become subjects of the English Crown; they were allies. They have never agreed to be subject to the government of Canada either. But as the settler population grew and became dominant, the Canadian government just assumed the power to govern the Haudenosaunee without ever obtaining their consent. The governing of a people without their consent is a primary feature of colonialism.

The non-Indigenous people of Canada have got to change their thinking about the various Indigenous peoples. They are separate nations that must be accommodated within the territory we know as Canada. The fact that we ignored this for 150 years does not change it, and justice demands it.

Woo's book explains that sovereignty includes the right to have traditional laws recognized. The Coronation Oath, taken by English kings from early times, was a vow by which the Crown accepted the loyalty of the people and undertook to protect them and govern them according to the "law of the land." The expression "law of the land" included the laws of the people to be governed. The government of Canada acquired authority through English common law and is bound to govern according to the laws of the land.

The treaties signed by Canada require that the Indigenous people be governed according to their own laws.

The treaties were made with the Indigenous people as independent nations, and those treaties are the basis of our relationship. As the newcomer population became more powerful and the Indigenous people were no longer needed as allies, the Department of Indian Affairs failed to observe those treaties, but legally their right to self-determination remains.

There are many people who say it is unworkable to have separate nations within one country, but this is in fact a reality we have tried to avoid until the present.

❖ II ❖

CROW DOG V. SPOTTED TAIL

White justice is punitive; Indigenous justice is restorative.
— The author

One of the best examples of the conflict between punitive justice and restorative justice is the 19th-century U.S. case *Crow Dog v. Spotted Tail* (*Ex parte Crow Dog*).

In traditional times, Indigenous people would use the restorative process even for charges as serious as murder. On August 5, 1881, Crow Dog shot and killed Spotted Tail. The circumstances surrounding the killing are vague. Both men were subchiefs in the Brulé Sioux nation. Crow Dog was a traditionalist and had fought in the Black Hills War, including the battle of the Little Big Horn. Spotted Tail was an accommodationist and did not fight in the war. This may have been a cause for bad blood between them. There is also some reference to Spotted Tail having taken Light-in-the-Lodge, the wife of Medicine Bear, a crippled man, into his household as his second wife, which may also have contributed to the animosity between himself and Crow Dog.

In any event, after the shooting, the matter was settled within the tribe according to long-standing tribal custom. Crow Dog was to make restitution to Spotted Tail's family in the sum of US$600 (about US$15,000 today), eight horses and one blanket. But, notwithstanding the settlement under tribal custom, Crow Dog was arrested and charged with murder under the laws of the Dakota Territory.

Crow Dog's defence argued that he had been tried and dealt with according to the customs of the Brulé Sioux, but Crow Dog was nevertheless tried and convicted. He was sentenced to be hanged on May 11, 1882. Notwithstanding this sentence, he was released to go home pending his appeal to the territorial Supreme Court. He returned to court as required, the conviction was confirmed and the execution was rescheduled for May 11, 1883.

Crow Dog successfully appealed to the Supreme Court of the United States. Justice Stanley Matthews delivered the judgment of the court and acquitted Crow Dog under a provision that said federal law shall not be construed to extend to crimes committed by one Indian against the person or property of another Indian, nor to any Indian committing any offence in Indian country who has been punished by the local law of the tribe.

In delivering the unanimous judgment of the Supreme Court, Matthews said:

> It tries them not by their peers, nor by the customs of their people, nor the law of their land, but by superiors of a different race, according to the law of a social state of which they have an imperfect conception and which is opposed to the traditions of their history, to the habits of their lives, to the strongest prejudices of their savage nature; one which measures the red man's revenge by the maxims of the white man's morality.

Unfortunately, the white population did not share the sentiments expressed by Justice Matthews. They wanted to assimilate the Indians into mainstream white society and do away with "heathen" tribal laws and apply their own law. So in 1885 Congress passed the Major Crimes Act, which brought seven major crimes under the jurisdiction of federal law. Amendments to that Act have increased that number to 15.

Wayne Ducheneaux, president of the National Congress of American Indians, testified before Congress on the matter in 1968:

Before all this came about we had our own method of dealing with law-breakers and in settling disputes between members. That all changed when Crow Dog killed Spotted Tail. Of
course, our method of dealing with that was Crow Dog should
go take care of Spotted Tail's family, and if he didn't do that
we'd banish him from the tribe. But that was considered too
barbaric, and thought perhaps we should hang him like civilized people do, so they passed the Major Crimes Act that said
we don't know how to handle murderers and they were going
to show us. (Quoted in Probasco 2001.)

As Larry Echo Hawk, a Pawnee who had been the Attorney
General of Idaho and was later Assistant Secretary of the Interior
for Indian Affairs, noted in 2000:

The Major Crimes Act was designed to give the federal
government authority to criminally prosecute seven specific
major crimes committed by Indians in Indian country. It was a
direct assault on the sovereign authority of tribal government
over tribal members.

At least the United States gave some recognition to tribal customs and laws. In Canada all authority over Indigenous people
was assumed by the Indian Act and the Indian agents. The
Criminal Code applied to all offences and there was no recognition given to Indigenous customs.

I see this as tremendously unfortunate because what I have
seen of the Indigenous customs has convinced me that the current justice system could be tremendously improved by following
those customs. Perhaps that will happen if we ever reach a truly
postcolonial era.

❖ 12 ❖

RUPERT ROSS

Probably one of the most serious gaps in the system is the dif-
ferent perception of wrongdoing and how best to treat it.
— Rupert Ross

I have received a fair amount of praise and acknowledgement for my efforts to understand the Indigenous people and apply the law in a culturally sensitive manner. I learned a great deal from Rupert Ross and from his books *Dancing with a Ghost* and *Returning to the Teachings*.

As a judge I dealt with many Indigenous offenders and listened to many Indigenous witnesses, but that didn't give me the opportunity to have conversations with them. I read many presentence reports which told of the family background of accused persons, and many of them spoke of relations of the accused who had been the victims of murder, fatal accidents and other alcohol-related deaths. One of the most poignant I recall was a young offender whose father was serving a life sentence for murder.

All of this made me aware of the horrendous social conditions that were causing such a disproportionate number of Indigenous people to come to my courtroom, but it did little to enable me to understand why or give me a clue as to how I might use the power of my office to effect change.

As a Crown lawyer in Kenora, Ontario, Rupert Ross was responsible for prosecutions in over 20 Cree and Ojibway communities. As such, he had a much greater opportunity to have conversations with witnesses and elders than I had as a judge, and I found his information and insights tremendously helpful.

Ross in turn acknowledges the help of Dr. Clare Brant, a psychiatrist who was a Mohawk from the Tyendinaga reserve:

> I will never forget reading some of his work for the first time, for it had the effect of suddenly making comprehensible a vast number of incidents which had always puzzled me. Without those keys, I would still be stumbling around in cross-cultural darkness unable to see any of the behavioural patterns that gave the traditional native worldview its unique structure.

That is how I felt when I read Ross's books. I quoted him extensively in judgments that brought me national and international media attention and earned me the reputation of being an advocate for better justice for the Indigenous people.

I discussed the use of Ross's material with him, and he warned me that his observations were with Cree and Ojibway people and might not apply to the First Nations in my jurisdiction. In my own observations and conversations with Stoney elders I found it was all very applicable. However, I acknowledge that I tend to be quite a bit more impulsive and insensitive than Ross. Perhaps that is what was necessary to shake things up at Morley in the mid-nineties.

In *Returning to the Teachings* Ross quotes an old Cree as saying, "You cannot pass along what another person really told you. You can only pass along what you heard."

That comment causes me sober reflection on my work as a judge. I wonder how many times I heard something that the speaker did not intend to say, or did not hear what he did intend to say. My thinking was significantly influenced by Rupert Ross, and I wish to acknowledge him for it. In relation to what he has said, I have the benefit of his written text. I still wonder how much of this I will manage to misinterpret.

In both of his books Ross quotes a justice proposal prepared by the Sandy Lake First Nation:

> Probably one of the most serious gaps in the system is the different perception of wrongdoing and how to best treat it. In the non-Indian community, committing a crime seems to mean that the individual is a bad person and therefore must be punished. ...The Indian communities view a wrongdoing as a misbehaviour which requires teaching or an illness which requires healing.

I find it interesting that he quotes this on page 71 of his first book, published in 1992, and on page 1 of his second one, which appeared in 1996. I wonder if that is an indication of his changing view of its importance, or if it is just because the first book is focused on cultural differences, the second on Indigenous justice.

In his introduction to the second edition of *Returning to the Teachings*, Ross says: "I never felt I had been able to escape my own paradigm enough to begin functioning freely in the other."

With his many years as a prosecutor it may have been more difficult for him to change his thinking than it was for me. He was an active player in the justice system for many years. In my career as a lawyer, I did a general practice with a fair amount of criminal defence work, but I was never as dedicated or enthusiastic about it as many of my colleagues were. When I was interviewed by the Judicial Council as a necessary step in my appointment as a judge, I was asked why I wanted to be a judge. My reply was that I didn't like being a player in the adversarial system and I thought I was better suited to being the referee.

As a judge I felt more like an observer than a participant, and when I began to see how the system was failing the Indigenous people, I had no real attachment to the system the way it was.

I took to heart things that Ross said, and in my impulsive and insensitive style I carried his ideas a step further.

In *Dancing* he says:

> We appear, for instance, to be on the verge of "discovering"
> that many varieties of antisocial behaviour may be caused, in
> ways not yet understood, by external influences such as high
> lead levels in air or water. Similarly, our social scientists are
> warning us that children who grow up in assaultive homes
> *learn* that behaviour and are to a large extent destined to
> repeat it in their own adult lives. Suggestions of this sort may
> well come to challenge our belief in individual free choice and
> responsibility to a significant degree.

I say it is obvious that much antisocial behaviour is caused by
external influences and that our reliance on the doctrine of free
choice is a cop-out by society in general that allows us to point
the accusing finger at wrongdoers and hold them individually
responsible for their wrongdoing, and thus avoid the societal
responsibility for the lack of social support that is a significant
factor in almost all wrongdoing.

I think the paragraph that had the most influence on my rejec-
tion of the concept of punishment was in *Dancing* where Ross
talks about a meeting he had with the council of a large reserve:

> I explained why we chose jail and fines as a response to
> criminal behaviour, outlining our view that such responses
> might prompt people to make different choices in the future.
> When the translator completed my explanation, there was
> what I can only describe as an excited but incredulous out-
> burst of comment from around the table. One elder exclaimed,
> "So that's why you do it!"

It was awe-inspiring to me to learn that the concept of punishment was so foreign to the understanding of these people. I
thought of all of the repeat offenders in my courts and the failure of prior punishments to change their conduct. I became

convinced that the Indigenous process was far superior to the system I had assumed was the only way to deal with antisocial conduct.

In *Returning*, Ross tells of a conversation he had with an Indigenous woman:

> "We know that you put him in jail for our protection, but to give us protection in that way, you'd have to keep him in there forever." Since that was not the case, she wondered why we couldn't support her healing way instead. If jail actually causes people to lose some of the coping, balancing, riding and steering skills they originally had, or to develop habits that make improving those skills harder still, then it only adds to their disabilities and to the misery of all.

This was a comment that impressed me when I first read this book 20 years ago. It reinforced my opinion about the futility of imprisonment.

I believe our whole criminal justice system is based on the erroneous assumption that it is necessary to control wrongdoing, and that this assumption is self-enforced by the adherence to precedent.

I have spoken of the gentleness that I see in Indigenous elders, and how it endears me to them. Ross talks about the different interpretation of "natural law" by Eurocentric people and by Indigenous people. The Eurocentric believe the natural law is exemplified by Darwin's theory of the survival of the fittest and that fierce competition guarantees the progress of mankind. The Indigenous view is the opposite, that "Creation demonstrates. at its most fundamental levels, principles of mutualism, interdependence and symbiosis. At those levels, all aspects of the created order are essential to the continued survival of Creation as a whole."

In his chapter "Watch Your Language" in *Returning*, Ross explains how English itself is harsher than Aboriginal languages.

English words are judgmental – "pest," "waste," "thief," "offender." We label people, but the labels "are usually only accurate if they are applied to a few narrow events taken from a few select moments in an individual's total life."

> ... And that's one of the reasons I shudder when I hear headlines screaming "Get Tougher on Those Offenders!" I don't know how to lock up and torture only the ugly "offender parts" of people while comforting the hurt parts, teaching the curious parts, nourishing the starved parts, unearthing the hidden parts, emboldening the cautious parts and inspiring the dreaming parts.

On the last page of *Dancing* Ross says: "… these people maintain an approach to existence that we might be wise to investigate."

I think this is a most delightful understatement. I am inclined to say that their approach to life produces a serenity that the Western world does not have, and we should study them and follow their example if we ever want to have real peace in our society.

❖ 13 ❖

PUNISHMENT

An eye for an eye would turn the whole world blind.
— Mahatma Gandhi

Why do we have punishment? In theory there are four purposes of punishment: deterrence, retribution, prevention and reform.

The deterrence theory says that if you punish someone for wrongdoing they will avoid further wrongdoing in order to avoid further punishment.

The retribution theory says that victims of crime will obtain some solace from seeing a wrongdoer also suffer.

The prevention theory says that threatened punishments will prevent would-be wrongdoers from doing wrong.

The reformative theory says that punishment will teach the wrongdoer not to repeat his wrongdoing.

These aspects of punishment were listed by John Salmond, a noted New Zealand jurist. He died in 1924, so his theories might be somewhat out of date.

The current Criminal Code of Canada was enacted in 1892 and was largely adopted from a proposed bill in England that was designed to codify their criminal law but was not in fact passed. The purpose of sentencing is stated in s. 718 (see chapter 1 of the present book). I certainly support the concept of the maintenance of the just, peaceful and safe society, but I am convinced that the methods are not working, specifically denunciation and deterrence.

The laws that were being codified went back hundreds of years before that proposed English bill, so we are still applying laws that were created long ago. Admittedly "thou shalt not kill" is somewhat timeless, but the archaic aspect of the Code is that it purports to reduce crime by methods that are likely contributing to the commission of crimes.

All serious (that is, indictable) offences specify the years of imprisonment to which the offender is liable. Most minor (summary conviction) offences specify a fine of up to $5,000 or six months imprisonment or both.

Section 731 allows a court to suspend sentence and direct that the offender be released on the conditions prescribed in a probation order.

Section 734 allows a court to impose a fine in lieu of imprisonment, unless there is a minimum period of imprisonment specified, in which case the court can impose a fine in addition to any minimum.

A Liberal government in 1996 attempted to reduce the use of imprisonment, by enacting 718.2(e):

> ... all available sanctions, *other than imprisonment* [italics mine] that are reasonable in the circumstances should be considered for all offenders, *with particular attention to the circumstances of aboriginal offenders* [italics mine].

Since the passage of the original Code we have learned a lot more about human psychology than what we knew in the 19th century. Wilhelm Wundt (1832–1920) is said to have established psychology as a separate field from philosophy, in 1879; Sigmund Freud (1856–1939) was advancing his theories on psychoanalysis by the turn of the century; and Carl Jung (1875–1961) was developing analytical psychology. The practice of psychiatry as a medical specialty in Western countries dates back to the mid-1800s.

So, in the last 150 years, while the basic principles of the

Criminal Code have remained pretty much the same, there have been huge advances in the fields of psychiatry and psychology.

Our growing knowledge of the human mind and human behaviour is telling us that punishments do not have the effect on modifying human behaviour that we have assumed they have.

Where did the idea of punishment come from?

The Christian Bible has had a huge effect on Western civilization and culture, and it seems to be all about punishment. Jesus is crucified for the sins of mankind. In Genesis, when Eve eats of the forbidden fruit she gets kicked out of the Garden of Eden. Cain murders Abel and is banished. (Interesting that he isn't executed.) In Numbers a man found gathering firewood on the Sabbath is stoned to death for violating the Sabbath.

In the Middle Ages kings were said to rule by "divine right." Every offence in England was "a breach of the King's peace." The king ruled in the place of God, so any offence was an offence against God and God "punished" wrongdoing.

Is our real objective in sentencing "to contribute … to respect for the law and the maintenance of a just, peaceful and safe society" (as is stated in the preamble to the sentencing sections), or is it just "punishment"?

If it is to contribute to respect for the law and the maintenance of a just, peaceful and safe society, there are much better ways of doing that than punishment. If the objective is just to punish, we should accept that it does very little good and wastes billions of dollars and destroys lives.

If we are doing it out of a Bible-based belief, are we not in fact using imprisonment to enforce the religious faith of that portion of our society that still believe in the application of the Bible? Does this mean that people who are imprisoned because of the Bible-based belief are religious prisoners? If we are imprisoning people because of Bible-based beliefs, is that not an infringement on the prisoner's right to freedom of religion?

There is no question that there are people who have such violent criminal tendencies that incarceration is the only way the public can be protected from them. But they are a very small portion of our prison population. A 1994 pamphlet by Ruth Morris entitled "But What About the Dangerous Few?" estimated that the really dangerous inmates of the Canadian prison system are about 1 or 2 per cent of the total population.

Dr. Ruth Morris (1933–2001) was a Canadian social activist, an author and a Quaker who advocated prison abolition and was a founding member of the International Conference on Penal Abolition.

The Quakers (Society of Friends) are a Christian sect that apply Jesus's teaching to love one's enemies by refusing to engage in physical combat – from claiming conscientious objector status during times of war, to refusing to pay taxes that are used for military purposes. The Quaker community won the Nobel Peace Prize in 1947.

I don't remember how I came into possession of the pamphlet, but I do recall reading it in my office in Canmore. It is a second printing from 1996, and that is probably about the time I received it. Over the last 20 years I have moved office and residence a number of times and purged the paperwork and books in my possession quite drastically. But I have kept "But What About the Dangerous Few?" and I agree with everything Morris says in it. I wish I had paid more attention at the time so I could have met her before she died.

She talked about "healing justice" and said she was often asked what she would do with the serial killer. Her first suggestion was to understand our own fears, and that the fear of the serial killer should not justify our retributive justice system.

This has certainly been my experience. I advocate for restorative justice and I am often challenged with the question What do you do with people like Paul Bernardo and Karla Homolka?.

One answer to that is another question: How many more horrible criminals can you name? Robert Pickton? Clifford Olson? Marc Lepine? Allen Legere? Alexandre Bissonette? There were more than 14,000 prisoners in Canadian federal penitentiaries in 2016/2017. We treat them all like the worst of them, and we don't even want them to reform.

Speaking of the worst, Karla Homolka would certainly rate as one of those, and yet she has remarried, had three children and seems to be leading the life of a typical soccer mom. The media reports reflect the disgust many feel over the fact that she is allowed to have a normal life after the evil things she did. Those are an indication that we don't actually want the reformation of serious criminals. Our cruel, unforgiving society wants them to suffer forever. Perhaps Karla Homolka is just a really good example of the fact that there is hope that even the worst of criminals can reform.

In Norway the maximum penalty is 21 years. It can be increased indefinitely in five-year increments, but the onus is then on the government to show that the prisoner still poses a threat to society. Norway provides some of the most humane treatment for prisoners in the world and has one of the lowest rates of recidivism, at 16 per cent. Conversely the United States, which emphasizes retribution over rehabilitation and has the largest percentage of prisoners in the world, has recidivism of 40 per cent. Even Anders Breivik, who murdered 77 people, including 69 youth at a summer camp, was only sentenced to 21 years.

But I have digressed. Back to Ruth Morris and "But What About the Dangerous Few?" She points out that eight times as many homicide victims are killed by family or friends as by street crime:

> So our first challenge is to look at the violent few in a realistic context. Their actions are terrible and terrifying, but they are not a major source of violence in our society.

She advocates more focus on the real causes of violence: the acceptance of the abuse of women in families, families in crisis, media violence and ready access to guns. The prevention of family violence, early intervention with children who have learning disabilities and behaviour problems, reduction of media violence, and gun control are four steps necessary to create a society which produces fewer serial killers.

Morris also advocates humane treatment of the dangerous few, separating them from other offenders but providing them with treatment and re-education, and holding them in small, personalized environments so they can recover from any abuse suffered in their childhood, which is often a contributing factor to violent behaviour in adults.

Her conclusion is this:

> The dangerous few are a symptom of the pathology of violence in our society. Our present response to them, using their existence as a reason for expanding a retributive justice system which embodies and creates violence, is completely counterproductive. Fear of the dangerous few is entirely normal and healthy. Let us use that fear to mobilize ourselves to root out the causes of violence in our society and build a caring community that nurtures and includes all.

In her book *Stories of Transformative Justice*, Morris makes this statement:

> Transformative justice sees crime as an opportunity to build a more caring, more inclusive, more just community. Safety doesn't lie in bigger fences, harsher prisons, more police or locking ourselves in till we ourselves are prisoners. Safety and security – real security – come from building a community where because we have cared for and included all,

that community will be there for us when trouble comes to us. For trouble comes to us all, but trouble itself is an opportunity.

If I had read Ruth Morris in 1977 when I was first appointed a judge I probably would have laughed her off as a total crackpot. My years of immersion in the criminal justice system opened my eyes to its futility. Today I see Morris's teachings as a beacon of wisdom and hope.

❖ 14 ❖

DETERRENCE

No punishment has ever possessed enough power of deterrence to prevent the commission of crimes.
— Hannah Arendt, *Eichmann in Jerusalem:*
A Report on the Banality of Evil

The single greatest justification of our use of punishment in the penal system is deterrence – the theory that if we punish people for wrongdoing, they will avoid the wrongdoing in order to avoid the punishments. We don't use the word "retribution" a lot because it sounds too biblical and vengeful. Although the system actually is all about retribution and vengeance, we like to talk about it as if we are really nice folks who only resort to punishment out of absolute necessity.

For the first 20 years that I sat as a judge I thought deterrence was a good thing. I would sentence people to long periods of imprisonment and feel good about it because I thought I was doing the public a service.

Rupert Ross, in his book *Returning to the Teachings*, says this about deterrence:

> It's strange, when you think of it, the determination we have in the Western justice system to make sure that those who are in charge of it have absolutely no personal knowledge of the forces haunting the people who are paraded daily before them. I often wonder how much of the judge's, a jury's or a lawyer's reliance on deterrence, for instance, comes from the fact that

they know *they* would be deterred by the possibility of certain punishments. As I've come to realize, however, there are a vast number of circumstances in which those punishments are not nearly as threatening to the poor, the hurt, the hopeless, the sick and the desperate.

During the years that I heard cases from the Indigenous community, I began to see the same people I had sentenced to lengthy periods of imprisonment coming back. They did their time and they reoffended. Almost all of the presentence reports I received showed a record of prior, similar offences. Often the accused had already served a prison sentence for the same behaviour I was sentencing them for again.

We know that many Indigenous nations did not use incarceration and yet their societies were peaceful. I say we use imprisonment far too much in Western society. The USA uses it more than any other country in the developed world. With less than 5 per cent of the world's population they have about 20 per cent of the world's prisoners, and their society is one of the most violent in the world. There are roughly three times as many murders per capita in the United States as there are in Canada, and mass shootings are becoming commonplace. When are we going to see the folly of it?

I referred earlier to a case in which I sentenced a man to three years in federal penitentiary for a vicious assault on his wife. He served the mandatory two-thirds of his sentence and was paroled two years later. He went right back to settle the score. The sentence apparently had no deterrent effect at all.

In the terrible case of *R. v. Blanchard* (referred to in chapter 9), the convicted had served a total of 34 years in prison. If there was ever going to be a situation where we had specific deterrence, was this not it? He was released with warnings to the public that he was a danger, and he committed another rape.

After 33 years of watching the gong show in my courtrooms, I have come to the unshakable opinion that deterrence is a legal fiction.

The term I like to use for it is "cognitive distortion," a term I got from my friend Bob Fulton, who explains it as follows:

> That term was coined by a psychologist to describe beliefs and rationalizations that patients suffering from depression construct to validate their feelings. The cognitive distortion is not true, but is keenly defended because their feelings are validated by the thought
>
> The process in clinical depression has a parallel in criminal justice. Serious crime, especially crimes of violence and sexual assault, elicit strong feelings in families of the victims and in the public forum. A large group of people react to serious crime by seeking retaliation through the Justice system. They rationalize this desire for revenge by thinking that it will deter others from acting like this in the future. It makes the public feel good to "save lives" while it satisfies its dark feelings. This is a cognitive distortion because it doesn't save lives or deter anyone in the future. In fact, the state-sponsored retaliation merely conditions the culture to accept violence as a legitimate method of conflict resolution.

I believe that as a society we have convinced ourselves that punishment produces deterrence, when actually it doesn't. It is a rationalization that society uses to justify using the criminal justice system to vent anger, hatred and vengeance against those who commit crimes. Since we don't want to admit that these are our real motives, we convince ourselves that we do it for the purpose of deterrence. We have been so successful in convincing ourselves of this that we believe it, but the empirical evidence says it does not work.

It is a distortion that costs billions of dollars and destroys countless human lives.

I estimate that 99 per cent of the violent offences I dealt with were alcohol-related. Our punitive justice system seeks to deal with many of these crimes with incarceration. The imprisonment is depressing. The depression of the offender is aggravated and thus the likelihood of reoffending is increased by the imprisonment rather than reduced by it.

This brings me to another fiction or urban legend: that Indigenous people do not have the same tolerance for alcohol as non-Indigenous people. My understanding is that there is no clinical or medical evidence that establishes this. It is true that we see a tremendous problem with alcohol abuse amongst Indigenous people, and the "no tolerance for alcohol" explanation is a comfortable rationalization by the dominant society because it takes away our responsibility. The real explanation, however, is that most people who abuse alcohol do so because they are self-medicating depression. Canadian colonialism has made the lives of Indigenous people so depressing that there is more alcohol abuse among them because there is more depression to be self-medicated.

If even a fraction of the money we so willingly spend on imprisonment were spent on the treatment of underlying causes instead, we would see a significant reduction in the offending behaviour and a considerable improvement in the quality of life of the offenders.

I have had occasion, in both my professional and my personal life, to try to find treatment for alcoholics. My experience is that there is very little available in Alberta or Canada. Provincial governments make millions from the tax on alcohol and spend a negligible amount on treatment for alcoholism, and the treatment centres that are available are not able to boast a very impressive success rate.

If a small portion of the amount that is currently spent on prisons were spent on addiction centres and counselling for addicts, the lives of the recovering addicts would be greatly improved, the crimes they commit would be reduced or eliminated, and many of the deaths and injuries caused by impaired drivers would be avoided.

As I have said, imprisonment has a place. The dangerous few do exist and the public has to be protected from them. Blanchard should have been kept in prison forever, not to punish him but to protect the public from him.

The only use of imprisonment should be the containment of those who pose a danger to the public. However, in our system we have thousands of people "doing time" because we engage in the cognitive distortion that this will "deter" them and others ʿrom offending behaviour. Milt Harradence, one of Canada's top criminal lawyers, who also served as a member of the Alberta Court of Appeal, described it as sacrificing them on the altar of deterrence. In my observation it does that, but it does very little to reduce crime.

While I was writing this, my friend Bob Fulton also referred me to an article by Lawrence W. Sherman entitled "Domestic Violence and Defiance Theory: Understanding Why Arrest Can Backfire."

Sherman advances the premise that the same remedy will have different results with different people. Specifically, that arrest and detention will reduce the recidivism with some people but may increase it with others. More socially bonded people are more deterrable; unemployed and unmarried people are least likely to be deterred by arrest:

> The finding that unemployed domestic violence suspects become more violent when arrested, while employed suspects become less violent, is now one of the most firmly established

empirical facts in the entire literature on the effects of criminal sanctions.

Sherman explains that there are four key concepts in the emotional response to experiences of sanctions: legitimacy, social bond, shame and pride. Whether or not a perpetrator will be deterred by sanctions will be determined by his view of the legitimacy of the sanctioning body, the social bond the wrongdoer has with the sanctioning body, the shame the offender feels and the pride he has in the aftermath of the sanction.

If the offender feels the sanctioning body is illegitimate, that he has weak bonds to the sanctioning community, that his shame goes unacknowledged and he becomes proud of his isolation from the community, the sanctions will provoke defiance and will in fact increase his wrongful behaviour.

This article helped me understand what I was doing in relation to the Indigenous offenders in my jurisdiction, or at least articulated it. I wouldn't have been able to state it the way Sherman has done, but it was my position that if the Indigenous people were going to respect the law, they had to be involved in it. That was my main motive for attempting to use sentencing circles. In doing so I believe I was practising what Sherman has described. The participation of members of the community would give legitimacy to the law being enforced; the offender would be answering to members of his own community and would hopefully have a bond with them; he would feel shamed, but if it was a reintegrative shame that would allow him to reconcile with the community, his pride would be restored.

My two main explanations of the disproportionate number of Indigenous accused coming into my courtroom had been that they were committing offences because of the dysfunctional community they lived in, and that non-Indigenous law enforcement officers may have been more likely to charge Indigenous people than other offenders. Sherman's analysis gives me a third explanation: that the Indigenous people did not respect the law I was enforcing – they did not accord it legitimacy.

❖ 15 ❖

DUE PROCESS

When you consider the vast power of the state and the min-
uscule power of the individual, you have to have something
which balances that power, and that is due process.
— Dr. Max Wyman

In 1975 the Alberta government created a commission to inquire
into "The Administration of Justice in the Provincial Court of
Alberta." One of the commissioners was Max Wyman, and I
remember being impressed by a talk he gave in which he discussed due process. At the time, in my pre-paradigm shift days, I
embraced the concept.

Due process is all of the rights an accused person has in the
criminal justice system, and their purpose is to protect the innocent from wrongful punishment. These rights are enshrined in
the Charter of Rights as follows:

7. Everyone has the right to life, liberty and security of the
    person and the right not to be deprived thereof except in
    accordance with the principles of fundamental justice.
8. Everyone has the right to be secure against unreasonable
    search or seizure.
9. Everyone has the right not to be arbitrarily detained or
    imprisoned. ...
11. Any person charged with an offence has the right

    a) to be informed without unreasonable delay of the
        specific offence;

b) to be tried within a reasonable time;

c) not to be compelled to be a witness in proceedings against that person in respect of the offence;

d) to be presumed innocent until proven guilty according to law in a fair and public hearing by an independent and impartial tribunal;

e) not to be denied reasonable bail without just cause;

f) except in the case of an offence under military law tried before a military tribunal, to the benefit of trial by jury where the maximum punishment for the offence is imprisonment for five years or a more severe punishment;

g) not to be found guilty on account of any act or omission unless, at the time of the act or omission, it constituted an offence under Canadian or international law or was criminal according to the general principles of law recognized by the community of nations;

h) if finally acquitted of the offence, not to be tried for it again and, if finally found guilty and punished for the offence, not to be tried or punished for it again; and

i) if found guilty of the offence, and if the punishment for the offence has been varied between the time of commission and the time of sentencing, to the benefit of the lesser punishment

I absolutely agreed with this concept in 1975 and for the first 20 years that I sat as a judge. My function was to protect the innocent from wrongful punishment, and if the application of the safeguards meant that accused persons who were guilty of the offence had to be found not guilty because of the technical nature of the application, that was okay too. It meant the same system would work when there was an innocent accused. I acquitted lots of people, but I don't think I ever had a case where the accused was actually innocent of any wrongdoing in the matter.

I thought the system was great. I remember being so impressed by a comment made by a Chief Justice of the Supreme Court of Alberta (now called the Court of Queen's Bench), James Valentine Hogarth Milvain: "Law is the grease on the wheels of civilization. Without the rule of law we have the law of the jungle."

What this meant to me was that the system would prevent unlawful punishment. I began to question the system when I learned that punishment was perhaps not the best way to effect behaviour modification, and perhaps not even a good way.

The law of the jungle is: "The strong take what they want and there is no protection for the weak." I became totally disillusioned by the system when I learned that the treatment of the Indigenous people of Canada by the government of Canada and its justice system was pretty much the application of the law of the jungle.

The downside of due process is the time it takes. All of the protections in the Charter require time: time to get a lawyer, time to prepare for trial, time to make full answer and defence, time to carefully examine every step taken by the police to ensure that none of the rights of the accused have been violated. All of this time involves highly paid lawyers and judges and support staff costing billions of dollars. Why do we spend all of this money? To ensure that no one who is accused of an offence is deprived of life, liberty and security of the person (i.e., no one is punished) without due process.

So, supposing we did away with punishment and just focused on solving problems? When Crow Dog killed Spotted Tail, the Sioux community apparently didn't even talk about what punishment should be imposed on Crow Dog. They focused on solving a problem. The death of Spotted Tail left his family without support, so the solution was to require Crow Dog to provide horses and blankets and financial support to his family. Moral judgment and biblical punishment did not enter into it.

❖ 16 ❖

SAWBONNA

I do healing work, but have been stuck in the place of not being able to
release this horror, and now I know that a new beginning is here.
— Margot Van Sluytman

The very idea of forgiving a murderer might seem repugnant to many in our Western society, but that is because we have been conditioned by the culture that has grown out of our cruel and vicious past.

A good example of the power, and the benefit, of forgiveness is the story of Margot Van Sluytman and Glen Flett.

On March 27, 1978, Flett and two others robbed a Brink's truck that was transporting money from the Hudson's Bay store in Scarborough, Ontario. Theodore Van Sluytman was a salesman at the store. Flett shot and killed him in the course of the robbery. He was convicted of second-degree murder, sentenced to life in prison and served 14 years before being released on parole.

Margot Van Sluytman was 16 at the time of the incident. Her family had moved to Canada from Guyana when she was 8, because they thought Canada was a safer place to live. Her family was close knit and life was reasonably comfortable until that dreadful day. Her mother became so depressed by the death that Margot moved out three months later because she found the atmosphere in their home so oppressive. Her life was completely changed by her father's murder and she went from one thing to another trying to find meaning in life, at one point becoming so depressed that she attempted to end her life by taking a whole bottle of Tylenol. Fortunately she changed her mind and called her uncle, who took her to a hospital and had her stomach pumped. She found some solace in writing, mostly poetry, and published her work online on what she called The Palabras Press. She also became active in the National Association for Poetry Therapy.

Flett served the beginning of his sentence in Millhaven Institution, a maximum security prison in Bath, Ontario, where his attitude toward life continued to harden and he had no thoughts to make any recompense for what he had done. Then he was transferred to Kent Institution, a maximum-security facility in Agassiz, British Columbia, where, in an experimental program, guards wore civilian clothes, called him by his name and treated him "like a person."

He says that at first he didn't like it very much – that he preferred Millhaven, where "the guards were the guards and I was the prisoner and we hated each other." But his attitude began to soften in Kent. While there he started a program he called LINC (Long-term Inmates Now in Community), which works to support perpetrators as well as victims of crime.

In 1992 Flett was released on parole. He became an outspoken advocate of restorative justice and spoke at schools and universities. Among other restorative justice efforts, he runs Emma's Acres, a farm in Mission, B.C., where victims and perpetrators of crime work side by side, growing vegetables. He says the labour and teamwork needed to make things grow is an ideal process for both sides to find mutual support and healing. He promotes restorative justice as part of his own quest for reconciliation.

In her book *Sawbonna: I See You, A Real Life Restorative Justice Story*, Margot describes the intense emotion of their first contact. This began with a donation made by Sherry Edmunds-Flett, Glen Flett's wife, to Margot's press. Sherry had chosen to do this upon reading about an award Margot received from the National Association for Poetry Therapy for her work creating and teaching courses as well as publishing books about how therapeutic writing can offer a way to deal with seemingly insurmountable pain. In an e-mail to Sherry, part of a lengthy correspondence, Margot had asked for an apology from Glen.

In his first letter to Margot directly, Glen said, "I don't expect you to ever forgive me but I so hope that your wounds are healing…"

Margo replied, "I do not use the word forgive; because it is too vast, it implies too many things for me." She concluded by saying, "I have a deep sense that both you and I will move on in our journeys in a deeper manner from this day, Glen Flett. I do healing work, but have been stuck in the place of not being able to release this horror, and now I know that a new beginning is here."

This was 29 years after the murder of her father – 29 years of sadness and confusion about life – and she finally began to feel a new beginning.

Flett had already experienced the inner conversion that was giving him some peace, and this seems to have come largely from the process at Kent where he was spoken to with respect. He said his first dealing with police was at age 7. I can't help wondering whether, if those officers back then had shown Glen the same respect that he was shown by the guards at Kent, he would have changed right then and Theodore Van Sluytman might still be alive.

Margot and Glen now both work to promote restorative justice, using the word "Sawbonna" for their experience and their work together. Five years after their meeting, Margot, then aged 50, completed a master's thesis entitled "Sawbonna: Justice as Lived Experience." Together and separately, she and Glen give talks about the importance of shared humanity as it relates to dealing with crime. Both work diligently to have an impact on the justice system. Margot has shared conversation with Archbishop Desmond Tutu about Sawbonna and victim voice. She has shared with inmates in Pollsmoor Prison, where Nelson Mandela was held for eight years. And she continues to be invited to have conversations with Canadian politicians about the fact that "retributive justice is not victim's services," while focusing on teaching about restorative practices. Margot and Glen are an amazing example of the healing power of forgiveness and the benefits of reconciliation to both offenders and victims.

Our criminal justice system judges people to be bad people and convinces many of them that they are. It just throws them away like garbage. The practice at Millhaven did this. The much more enlightened process at Kent produced a much better result.

Chief Seattle is often credited with having said: "We did not weave the web of life. We are but strands within it. Whatsoever we do to the web, we do to ourselves."

Glen Flett is a strand in the web, and the web is stronger for his transformation. Margot Van Sluytman too is a strand in the web, and the web is stronger for her transformation.

Our society as a whole would be better if we did more to produce transformations like this.

❖ 17 ❖

REV. DALE LANG

The problem will be if you can't reach that place of forgiveness, then you're going to get stuck in that place of anger and bitterness.
— Rev. Dale Lang

Another amazing story of forgiveness is one that begins with a school shooting in Taber, Alberta, on April 29, 1999, just eight days after 13 students were killed at Columbine High School in Littleton, Colorado.

The shooters in both cases were said to have been bullied at school and this was apparently their motivation.

The Taber shooter is reported to have talked about the Columbine incident with approval and his was a copycat killing. He shot and killed Jason Lang, a 17-year-old student at W.R. Myers High School. Jason's parents are the Reverend Dale and Diana Lang.

Reverend Lang forgave the 14-year-old who committed this random act of violence. The shooter did not know Jason; he just wanted to kill someone and Jason was the unfortunate victim.

Since the shooting Dale Lang has spoken hundreds of times to encourage people to forgive. He speaks about how a normal spring day changed so drastically with the phone call telling him his son was in the hospital and he should come immediately. At the hospital he was told of the shooting and that his son did not survive. He describes the horrible pain and anger he experienced at the loss, but says his thoughts about the shooter were that he must be a very damaged young man.

At the memorial service held at the school five days after the shooting, Lang asked the people of Taber to support the family of the shooter. He told the gathering that they too would be suffering from the terrible tragedy and it would be wrong if they were to be harassed by the community.

The part of his message that most impressed me was the idea that forgiveness brings freedom.

Lang tells the story of a woman who came up to him after one of his talks and said she thought it was unbelievable that he could forgive the man who killed his son. Her son had been killed by an impaired driver 15 years earlier and she was still angry.

Lang's anecdote illustrates that this woman was still imprisoned by her own anger, while Lang was free because he had let go of his.

The other part of Reverend Lang's message is that forgiveness breaks the cycle of violence.

I lament the violence in our society, both here in Canada and in the much more violent United States. I blame the criminal justice system as a significant causal factor in this lamentable situation. I believe the cruel and oppressive criminal system contributes to the violence by teaching people that vengeance is okay.

I believe that capital punishment contributes to the murder rate by teaching people that if you really don't like someone, it is okay to kill them. My theory is supported by the fact that in the U.S., states that have the death penalty show higher murder rates than those that do not.

It is also interesting to note that the U.S. incarceration rate is more than five times that of Canada, something that also seems to correlate with their greater murder rate.

If there were a greater emphasis on forgiveness than on vengeance, I believe the whole of society would become more peaceful.

❖ 18 ❖

TO FORGIVE OR NOT TO FORGIVE

The weak can never forgive. Forgiveness is the attribute of the strong.
— Mahatma Gandhi

I have recently become acquainted with Annette Stanwick, the author of *Forgiveness: The Mystery and Miracle*.

In the book, she tells of the murder of her brother Soren and all the emotion she went through as a result, starting with the fateful phone call from her brother Rick telling her the news.

Soren was a long-distance truck driver who lived in Idaho. He was found shot dead in his rig in Richmond, Virginia. For more than a year it was a complete mystery as to why it happened, and then the FBI called to say they had arrested a mother and her three sons in a similar incident in which another trucker had been murdered.

Stanwick tells of the shock and the grief, that she kept looking for him in all the trucks they passed as they drove to Idaho for the funeral. She tells of listening to the song "(God is Watching Us) From a Distance" as they drove, and breaking down with anger toward God for letting this happen to her brother. She was also angry with the murderer, though they did not yet know who that was.

At the funeral she and her brothers shared Soren's poetry and their thoughts, memories and sorrows in front of the large number of people who had gathered there.

Her mother sat in the front row watching them with disbelief.

Annette's father had died of a massive heart attack at age 52. Her mother never got over it and suffered from the loss for the rest of her life. Annette says she remembers her mother saying with clenched teeth and fists: "I will never get over the death of your father." She goes on to say she now sees that her mother made a choice – the choice to never get over it. Annette's choice was to recover and that is what she has done.

She speaks of her relationship with God – that God told her that the man who murdered her brother was deeply troubled.

When the arrest was made in the similar incident a year later, further investigation showed that the perpetrators were in fact the ones who had killed Soren in an attempt to steal his truck. One of them, Travis Friend, pleaded guilty. Annette and her family travelled to Virginia for the sentencing and to provide victim impact statements.

In the course of the proceeding they heard about Travis and listened to a tale of 25 years of abuse and unfaithfulness inflicted by Travis's father on his wife and three sons; that he had lived in loneliness, shame and poverty; and that the whole family was wounded. Annette felt compassion for him in spite of what they had done to Soren and others.

In her victim impact statement, Annette told Travis about her close family, about her role in raising her brothers because her mother was unable to provide all the care they needed, and about the devastation he had caused by taking Soren from them. In her conclusion she said: "Here in the quietness of this moment I am offering God's love and forgiveness to you, Travis, and I am also offering you my love and forgiveness." She went on to encourage Travis to seek help from the prison chaplain.

When the proceeding was over Travis was sentenced to life imprisonment with no parole, but Annette left the courtroom with the freedom that came from letting go of her anger, hatred and need for vengeance.

I personally believe forgiveness does much more good for the forgiver than it does for the forgiven. In fact, my friend Bob Fulton tells me it may actually not be a good thing to forgive a wrongdoer who has not asked for forgiveness, because if they receive it without asking for it, it may seem to them that their action has been condoned. It is when a wrongdoer feels the separation shame causes and then is reintegrated by forgiveness that they benefit.

The importance of Annette's lesson is that she experienced a benefit from what she did.

The other side of this coin was sadly demonstrated by the case of Terri-Lynne McClintic.

On April 8, 2009, 18-year-old McClintic and her 28-year-old boyfriend, Michael Rafferty, kidnapped and murdered 8-year-old Tori Stafford in Woodstock, Ontario.

The horror of the offence they committed cannot be overstated. Terri-Lynne befriended Tori as she was leaving school and pulled her into Rafferty's car. They drove to a secluded place where he raped the little girl and Terri-Lynne murdered her with a claw hammer that Rafferty had told her to purchase, apparently for that purpose.

Terri-Lynne pleaded guilty to first-degree murder in 2010 and was sentenced to life imprisonment with no possibility of parole for 25 years.

Her prison classification was changed to medium security in 2014 and she was subsequently transferred to the Okimaw Ohci Healing Lodge in Saskatchewan. On September 25, 2018, Tori Stafford's father protested the move and arranged a demonstration against it on Parliament Hill. The Conservative opposition introduced a motion in Parliament to condemn the transfer to the healing lodge. The motion was defeated 200 to 82, with the NDP and the Green Party supporting the Liberals.

Although the Conservative motion was unsuccessful, Corrections Canada subsequently transferred McClintic back to an Ontario prison.

The opposition to treatment for Terri-Lynne is a graphic demonstration of the punishment-minded attitude of a portion of our population.

If Tori Stafford had died a horrible death by falling from a bridge through a defective guardrail, landing on rocks below and lying there suffering for hours but dying before she could be saved, the reaction of reasonable people would be to fix the bridge so this wouldn't happen to anyone else.

Tori died because Terri-Lynne McClintic was the defective rail. The story of her life made her defective. She was born to a stripper who didn't want her and gave her to fellow stripper Carol McClintic. Carol McClintic's two natural children had been apprehended by social services because she was an unfit mother, but she was nevertheless allowed to adopt Terri-Lynne, who was abused throughout her childhood. The abuse allegedly included being raped many times by her adoptive mother's boyfriends. At the time of the murder her mother was in the business of selling drugs, and by coincidence Tori's mother was one of her customers and was there purchasing drugs while Tori was being abducted.

From this home situation, Terri-Lynne ends up in the company of a man 10 years older than she is. He wants her to join him in a kidnapping, and she does. She says she walks away from the car when he is so horribly abusing the girl and then in those circumstances she smashes the child's head with the hammer, killing her. I wonder if she wasn't motivated by a desire to end the suffering for this unfortunate little girl.

If there was ever a young girl who was in need of a healing lodge it was Terri-Lynne McClintic. She is a broken person who badly needs help. I applaud the person in Corrections Canada for the decision to send her to that healing lodge, and I lament the decision to remove her from it.

I watched an interview with Tori's mother, Tara McDonald, in which she said she had expected she would feel differently after the legal proceedings and the sentencing, but she didn't. She also said Terri-Lynne could apologize until she died and she would never accept the apology. I believe that the reason McDonald didn't feel any differently after the sentencing is because, for her to feel differently, to feel the release that an Annette Stanwick, for example, felt, she herself would have to change.

She also has to forgive herself. Bob Fulton explained to me that the inability to forgive another comes from the inability to forgive yourself. Tara McDonald must feel terrible recriminations for being out buying drugs while her little girl was being abducted and murdered. Tori's father, Rodney Stafford, has been outspoken in his demands for tough treatment of Terri-Lynne McClintic, but he must feel self-recrimination for the fact that he had not exercised his visitation rights for six months before she died.

So everyone involved is miserable. What good does it do to punish Terri-Lynne? If our objective in criminal law is to protect society and maintain it as a just, peaceful and safe milieu, what contribution does keeping her in a cement cell achieve? To return to my bridge analogy, fixing the broken guardrail will prevent further deaths far more successfully than tearing it down.

❖ 19 ❖

ANGER, HATRED, VENGEANCE

*Anger is an acid that can do more harm to the vessel in which
it is stored than to anything on which it is poured.*

— Mark Twain

My friend Chris Evans co-edited an anthology titled *Tough Crimes*. He might not still call me a friend if he reads this book and especially this chapter. Chris was a Crown prosecutor for many years, then a defence counsel, and one of his favourite quips was: "Accused persons are innocent until proven broke." Chris is a very able lawyer who thinks the system is just fine the way it is. He is a good example of how difficult it is to change the thinking that could change the world.

Tough Crimes gathers 20 essays by top criminal lawyers on their most difficult cases. The case which to me was the most horrifying was written up by Fred Ferguson, a former Crown who was appointed a Provincial Court judge in 2003 and became a Queen's Bench justice in 2008.

His chapter, "John Ryan Turner," is the story of a little boy who died at the age of three years and nine months because of mistreatment and neglect by his parents. The neglect began right from birth, as the mother suffered from postpartum depression and failed to bond with the child. Apparently the father shared the mother's failure to bond, in a case of folie à deux, a malady that develops between two people as a shared psychosis. And not only was there neglect, there was evidence of restraints and gags having been used on the child. Though he had several untreated fractures, it was not shown he was deliberately injured; the broken bones may have been attributable to the restraints alone. In any event, it appears that when his parents couldn't deal with him they bound and gagged him.

The actual cause of death was very difficult to determine, but the child was ultimately diagnosed as suffering from a non-organic failure to thrive – the Kaspar Hauser syndrome of organic dwarfism.

Each parent was convicted of manslaughter and sentenced to 16 years in prison.

The cost of the trial must have been substantial. Ferguson recounts that there were 25 expert witnesses and that the reports filled banker's boxes. This together with other witnesses and the court time – salaries of the staff, the judge and lawyers – would have amounted to tens, perhaps hundreds, of thousands of dollars. Then the imprisonment would have cost hundreds of thousands more.

The total cost of the investigation, trial and imprisonment of the parents would have been in the millions of dollars.

Why?

Because what happened to that little boy makes us angry. We hate the people who did it to him and we want vengeance. So we spend millions of our multi-billion-dollar criminal justice budget to vent our anger, hatred and vengeance.

What good does it do?

We do it in the name of protecting society by deterring offenders and potential offenders. These parents were so totally useless that they could not even raise their own son. He died because of their uselessness, not because they are violent and pose a threat to anyone else. As far as deterring others is concerned, other similarly useless parents will probably never even know about this case.

We also do it to ease our own collective conscience. The parents were singled out and made to pay society's price for their neglect of that little boy.

But what about our responsibility as a society? Ferguson tells of contact with a number of agencies that were aware of the mother's postpartum depression and her difficulties with the child; about a public health nurse expressing concern to a doctor about the boy; a conversation in which the mother had told the public health nurse she couldn't deal with the boy's incessant crying; an anonymous call to the Child Protection Branch that was not acted on; neighbours and even the postman who expressed concerns but didn't make actual reports.

Ferguson ends his story by saying: "...it takes a man and woman to conceive a child but it takes a whole community to properly raise one." But he'd started the story by recounting a talk he had given in the community about the genesis of so many violent criminal personalities and the need to identify children at risk at an early age so as to better manage their needs through early intervention by people trained in social work and healthcare.

To me this is a lamentable inconsistency. Ferguson sees the need for early childhood intervention, but he is prepared to have millions spent on proving guilt and punishing parents while offering no suggestion as to how better to deal with the problem.

In my world parents such as John Ryan Turner's would attend a conference with social workers, neighbours, doctors and others to determine what could be done to repair the harm they have done, not just to their child but to the whole of society, which also suffers when offences such as this occur.

Instead of spending all that money to establish guilt and punish, funding would be increased for child welfare in the community. If there were extra childcare workers visiting every child in the community regularly, incidents like this would not happen and parents who just need a little help would get it. The benefits that can be derived by extra funding to the care of children are immeasurable, but we prefer to spend the money on venting our anger, hatred and vengefulness.

In a more recent case, in February 2017, in Calgary, Emil Radita, 60, and his wife, Rodica Radita, 54, were found guilty of the first-degree murder of their 15-year-old son, Alexandru Radita.

The boy was diabetic and he was so emaciated when he died in May 2013 that he weighed less than 37 pounds. He had been hospitalized in B.C. in October of 2003 and was near death, apparently as a result of his parents failing to treat his diabetes. After being discharged from hospital, he was apprehended by social workers and placed in care for about a year. He thrived while in foster care. A picture of him at the time he left care showed him to be a chubby, happy-looking 6-year-old.

In 2004 the Raditas applied to have Alexandru returned to their custody and back with their seven other children. In December of 2004 there was a child protection hearing before Provincial Court Judge Gary Cohen in Surrey, B.C. The province's Ministry of Children and Family Development sought a continuing custody order that would keep Alexandru in the permanent care of a foster mother. The problem was that the Raditas had not given him his insulin. But Judge Cohen believed that having seen the results of their failure and the result of proper care they would do better, so he returned the boy to his parents.

Following the hearing the Raditas moved to Calgary and discontinued Alexandru's treatment. He died as a result of bacterial sepsis brought on by extreme starvation that was the result of the untreated diabetes.

In the murder trial, Justice Karen Horner found that the Raditas intended to and did isolate Alex from anyone who could intervene or monitor his insulin treatment, and that his condition was not a sudden onset and must have taken place over months and possibly years. She found that his isolation was an unlawful confinement, and that their refusal to treat his medical condition with proper insulin protocol care, when they knew he was dying, was murder. She imposed the mandatory life in prison with no chance of parole for 25 years. Neither of them had a comment or showed any emotion during the sentencing.

Patricia MacDonald, the B.C. social worker who fought against Alex being returned to his parents, was in court for the verdict. She was quoted as having said: "I'm happy with the verdict. I think that it really is justice for Alex. He went through a horrible ending to his life and I'm glad to see his parents being held accountable." She added, "I just feel like they're so empty. They're void of any kind of emotion, any kind of feeling. I've never met parents like them in my life."

So, young Alex died because his parents didn't give him his insulin, and they were convicted of murder and sentenced to life in prison. There was a time when I would have totally agreed with what was done to them. It is easy to hate them for what they have done. They are people who let their son starve to death because without his insulin he couldn't get proper nutrition. Now, however, my feeling toward them is not anger or hatred, but rather compassion. I feel as much sorrow for them as I do for their deceased son.

For myself, loving my children was the greatest joy and the greatest privilege of my life. When they were little and they would cry, for whatever reason, it gave me great joy to be able to comfort them and hold them until they were happy again. Losing my son to cancer is the greatest sorrow of my life. To think that these people were unable to have natural feelings of love, to feel the need to protect their son and take every possible step to make him well, is simply proof that there was something missing in their humanity. They should be pitied for that rather than punished for it.

It does seem as though the Raditas were not completely devoid of feelings for their son. A photo of Alex just three months before he died, showing him to be so emaciated, was taken at a birthday party his parents reportedly had organized for him. Apparently they had some mental quirk that enabled them to deny the diagnosis of diabetes. There was also some suggestion they had refused to give him the insulin because of some religious conviction.

For me, one encouraging thing was the newspaper coverage with headlines such as "Can the Sad, Short Life of One Boy Save Others?" (*Calgary Herald*, November 4, 2017) and "System Failed Diabetic Teen, Says BC Child Advocate" (*Calgary Herald*, June 13, 2016). The latter story quoted Mary Ellen Turpel-Lafond, B.C.'s Representative for Children and Youth at the time, as saying: "When we have a kid like this, shouldn't there be an Amber Alert?"

Turpel-Lafond explained the very tenuous nature of the processes currently in effect and how easy it is for such notices to get overlooked in the recipient offices: "Hopefully someone sees it, but *these child welfare offices are frequently overworked and understaffed.*" She suggested there needs to be a system like the Canadian Police Information Centre, which enables law enforcement agencies to get access to information on a number of matters quickly.

I have added the emphasis in the above quotation of Turpel-Lafond because my absolute conviction is that we should be spending a lot more money on social services and a lot less on prisons. The average cost per inmate in federal prisons in Canada was $119,152 in 2014/15 for a total of $2.63-billion. If the Raditas actually do spend the next 25 years in prison, that will cost at least $6-million, not counting inflation, and they are just two of the thousands of prisoners who pose no danger to the general public. They are just people who have some mental quirk, or perhaps a religious belief, that has them refuse to provide insulin to a diabetic child.

In the utopian world I dream of, we would replace anger, hatred and vengeance with understanding, and we would do it by transferring billions from the criminal justice system to the social welfare system.

❖ 20 ❖

ADVOCACY VS. CONVERSATION

Yesterday's solution is today's problem.

— Peter Senge

In *Dancing with a Ghost* Rupert Ross tells of a conference he attended in 1986 in Whitehorse in which he first saw shortcomings of the adversarial process in relation to Indigenous offenders. In his usual gentle style he says: "It was commonly agreed by the conference participants that Native people, with their belief in consensus decision-making, might find our adversarial system foreign and inappropriate."

My view is that the adversarial system is wrong for everyone. As a judge I saw far too many cases lost by inept counsel or won by very able counsel when the proper result of the process would have been the opposite of what I was required to do.

Why do we have the adversarial system? I believe it goes back to the days of trial by combat when people actually believed that a fight to the death by men representing either side of an argument would determine the truth.

In my view, that system determined nothing else except the winner. The use of it in our justice system usually produces the same results.

Why do we have the right to remain silent? I believe that goes back to the days when the most sadistic tortures were used in order to get suspects to admit to a crime. After hundreds of years of this, people finally realized that suspects would say anything you wanted them to say if you subjected them to sufficient pain. So in order to prevent suspects from being tortured to make false confessions, they were given the right to remain silent.

This right to remain silent makes a ritual of denying responsibility for harmful behaviour. The system that allows an accused person to remain silent allows them to avoid responsibility.

Why do witnesses have to testify in the face of wrongdoers who may have seriously hurt them? That is because of Sir Walter Raleigh, a pirate and a murderer who was knighted by Queen Elizabeth I for his contributions to England, only to be beheaded later by King James I for disobeying an order that he avoid engaging with Spanish forces. At his trial Raleigh insisted he should be able to face his accuser, and thus began the practice of requiring witnesses to testify in the face of the accused. This has worked terrible hardships, especially on women who are the victims of violent sexual offences.

The alternative to this practice is found in the Indigenous process by which elders would speak separately to members of the community to determine what in fact happened. In their system this was not prone to injustice, because the object of the exercise was not to punish a wrongdoer but rather to solve a problem. They may well have been uninterested in exactly who did what to whom. They simply wanted to acknowledge a problem and find a way to deal with it.

When I attended the conference of the Institute for the Advancement of Aboriginal Women in 2017, I suggested an alternative to our way of dealing with domestic violence. Aboriginal women as a group are the most abused people in Canada, and those at the conference seemed to agree with my proposed alternative.

Currently when the police are called to a domestic disturbance, they typically discover that one of the parties has assaulted the other, usually the man the woman. They then arrest the one they suspect to be the offender and take him into custody. He is brought before a judge to speak to his release, and one of the usual release provisions is that he have no contact with the victim. He will retain a lawyer to deal with the charge, and the standard advice the lawyer will give is that the accused not say anything to anyone. If he pleads not guilty and the matter is set down for trial, so much time will have elapsed before they get to trial that they will hardly remember what happened.

In my system the police wouldn't even ask who did what to whom. They would simply determine that there was a problem between the parties involved. When someone has called them because people are fighting or yelling at each other in a violent manner, it is a reasonable conclusion that there is a problem. The police would simply tell the parties that they see a problem that requires the couple to separate for the night and they would ask them to decide who leaves. If neither of them has a place to go, the police would have a hotel room available where one of them could stay. Within a day or so the parties would attend a conference. They would be encouraged to invite anyone they thought might help them come to a resolution: their children, their parents, any friends who might be interested. They would then engage in a conversation with a trained facilitator. The object would be to define the problem and develop a program that would help the couple avoid further conflict.

This may seem like a utopian dream. One can easily imagine the objections based on cost. But when you consider the current cost of police, custodial confinement, court facilities and the salaries of all the judges and lawyers who will become involved, the cost savings that would be realized would more than pay for hotel rooms, meeting rooms and facilitators, and there would be huge benefits. Marriages might actually be saved and the lives of participants made better.

We will not solve today's problems by addressing them at the same level where they were created in the first place.

The punitive justice system was created in an age when fear was the only behaviour modification technique that was known to those who had the responsibility for keeping order in society. Punishments were used to make people afraid to disobey the law. This is the essence of deterrence.

Punishment became the given. It was assumed that punishment would deter wrongdoing and result in the peaceful, orderly society that governments wanted to achieve.

Wrongful punishment was agreed to be wrong, so steps had to be taken to ensure there would be no wrongful punishment.

In an age when most people were illiterate, it was necessary to have advocates who would speak for accused persons and help them understand the process. As literacy increased, so did the complications of the legal system, and so the necessity for lawyers was perpetuated.

As the system becomes more and more complicated and congested, there is a huge demand for more police, more prosecutors, more courtrooms, more money for legal aid lawyers. Then, of course, we also need more prisons and more guards.

The criminal justice system costs billions of dollars a year and I believe it does more harm than good. If we only imprisoned those offenders who are dangerous because of propensities that cannot be otherwise controlled, and used alternative methods for the rest, we could save billions of dollars and make the lives of offenders and victims, and therefore our entire society, better.

❖ 21 ❖

POLARIZATION

*Polarization affects families and groups of friends. It's
a paralyzing situation. A civil war of opinion.*

— Mick Jagger

On February 9, 2018, Gerald Stanley was acquitted of murder in the death of Colten Boushie.

On February 22, 2018, Raymond Cormier was acquitted of murder in the death of Tina Fontaine.

On February 24, 2018, Edouard Maurice shot and wounded Ryan Watson in an incident similar to the Stanley matter.

All three of these cases have been the subject of public demonstrations, and I see them as examples of how our criminal justice system polarizes Canadians and turns them against each other.

Colten Boushie had been out swimming with friends. They were on their way home when they apparently had a problem with one of the tires on the dilapidated old van they were driving. They drove onto the Stanley farm and a couple of the occupants of the van tried to start an ATV on the property. It is reasonable to assume they intended to steal it and use it to get home.

Gerald Stanley admitted to firing his Tokarev TT33, a semi-automatic pistol originally made for the Soviet Red Army. He says he fired it three times, but it only discharged twice, and that then, when he was reaching into the vehicle to take away the keys, it just went off again, "accidentally" sending a bullet into the back of Boushie's head and killing him. The "hang fire" theory was tenuous, but the all-white jury, trying the white man for killing an Indigenous youth, acquitted on the defence argument that the death was an accident.

The verdict resulted in demonstrations by Indigenous people across Canada in support of Colten Boushie. A GoFundMe campaign in support of Stanley raised over $200,000, while an international petition to stop the GoFundMe campaign garnered more than 12,000 signatures.

I see this unfortunate conflict in our society as a serious matter that will predictably lead to more violence if it is not brought under control.

The case of Edouard Maurice is a further example of the problem. When Ryan Watson and Stephanie Anne Martens came onto the Maurice property and were rummaging through vehicles, Maurice confronted them and fired a gun, hitting Watson and injuring his arm. Watson was admitted to hospital with non-life-threatening injuries and discharged.

Maurice was charged with aggravated assault, pointing a firearm and careless use of a firearm, while Watson and Martens were charged with trespassing by night and theft under $5,000.

When Maurice appeared in court there were over a hundred people demonstrating in his favour and a GoFundMe campaign apparently had raised more than $10,000 by then.

Many of the rural residents in the area expressed anger and frustration at charges being laid against Maurice because they said it deprives them of the right to defend themselves and their property.

This was Stanley's position as well, but in his case a crucial element became the allegations of racism. The victim was an Indigenous youth and he was acquitted by an all-white jury.

I don't like to think there is a lot of overt racism in Canada. When my chief judge ordered me moved out of the jurisdiction that had me dealing with Indigenous accused because I had "lost my objectivity" with them, I didn't think he was being anti-Indian. I believe he was just so convinced of the righteousness of his system that he resisted change.

I acknowledge that the Indigenous people suffer from the racism of the dominant society, but I like to believe it is not so much anti-Indian as it is the righteous belief that Canada is a good country, it has always been a good country and it continues to be a good country, and that anyone who says otherwise is just wrong.

The years I spent trying to understand the sources of social dysfunction in the Indigenous community showed me that Canada has not always been a good country. There are quotes in Hansard, the official record of the Canadian Parliament, that have our first prime minister, Sir John A. Macdonald, speaking of the need to preserve the Aryan race. I see his policies in relation to the Indigenous people as the genocidal policies of a white supremacist racist. So, I like to think that Canadians of today are not deliberately racist, but there is some latent racism as a result of what we have become because of the overt racism of our predecessors. This is certainly something we have to deal with and eliminate, and there are positive steps being taken to do this.

I don't think Gerald Stanley's acquittal had very much to do with racism in the criminal justice system. I think it just demonstrated the inadequacy of the system generally.

The system is not designed to *fix* things. The Criminal Code of Canada is a penal statute. It prescribes *punishment* for every wrongful act. There have been some changes over the years to emphasize rehabilitation and employ restorative justice concepts, but its primary purpose is still the punishment of wrongdoing.

The principal function of the police is to enforce the law. Their mandate is to arrest wrongdoers and gather evidence that will prove their guilt so that they can be punished. There have been efforts to change the emphasis in the mandate of the police from enforcement to service, but their main task is to use whatever force is necessary to stop wrongdoing.

The primary purpose of the court is to prevent wrongful punishment. In order to ensure that the state does not punish people wrongfully, we have what we call due process.

Due process requires that the police gather their evidence according to a strict set of rules, and provide that evidence to the Crown prosecutor, who then decides whether to lay charges and if so which ones. The charge must be specific so that the accused person knows exactly what they are facing. The Crown then has the task of proving the specific charge beyond a reasonable doubt.

So, in the Stanley case, the court system did exactly what it was supposed to do. It found that the evidence gathered by the police and presented by the Crown was insufficient to prove the specific charge of murder in the second degree. Gerald Stanley was therefore acquitted.

Was this justice?

Unfortunately, that will depend on your definition of that word.

If you think justice is the proper working of the so-called justice system, your answer should be yes.

If you want more from the system, your answer will be no.

So, what would have been justice for the victim, Colten Boushie? If Stanley had been convicted of murder and sentenced to life imprisonment with no parole for ten years, would it have made things better for Boushie's family and those who loved him? Some will argue it would have given them closure, but other than allowing them to vent their anger, hatred and need for vengeance, it wouldn't do much for them.

I suggest we could honour Colten Boushie, and all the other Indigenous people who have been wronged by the system, by changing the current system to a process that would forget punishment and produce resolution.

If my vision were to prevail, a community justice conference would have been held, attended by both the Boushie and the Stanley families along with their respective supporters and advisers, and the proceeding would have been a facilitated conference in which all aspects of the matter would be discussed. Stanley might speak of his insecurity in rural Saskatchewan and his near panic at the intrusion of Boushie and his friends. The Boushies might talk about their love for the deceased and what they had lost.

The discussion might result in the Boushies seeing that Colten and his friends were out of line and that Stanley did the best he could. It might result in Stanley seeing how wrong it was for him to have that Russian semi-automatic pistol and to use it as he did. He might offer to compensate by transferring a piece of land to the family. Whatever the resolution, the process would be peaceful.

In community justice conferences the object of the process is to come to an agreement that satisfies the victim(s) and with which the wrongdoer is willing to comply. The alternative of trial in the adversarial system resolves nothing and creates the danger of further violence.

As I said in chapter 5 on the origins of processes, the adversarial system comes from primitive times in England where they thought they could solve all problems by fighting about them. The primitive Indigenous people sought to solve problems by talking about them.

My critics will say that if Gerald Stanley committed an offence, then he must be punished, and that my process would allow people to commit criminal offences and get away without punishment, by compensating the victims.

Why do wrongdoers have to be punished? Just because Stanley was acquitted of murder, that does not mean he was innocent of any wrongdoing, but the acquittal does mean the criminal justice system will not be doing anything to mitigate the loss suffered by

Boushie's family. If Stanley had been convicted, his incarceration for the minimum of ten years would cost the taxpayers of Canada about a million dollars and it would still be doing nothing to mitigate the loss.

The acquittal of Raymond Cormier in the death of Tina Fontaine was far more an indictment of social services than of the justice system, but it was another case which garnered a lot of public attention and generated a lot of anger about missing and murdered Indigenous people.

Tina was from the Sagkeeng First Nation reserve in Manitoba, where she was raised by her great-aunt, Thelma Favel. Her father had been brutally murdered in the fall of 2011, severely beaten, tied up and left to die. Tina wrote a victim impact statement for the sentencing of the perpetrators in 2014, which her great-aunt said was very upsetting for the girl, then aged 15.

Tina did well in school and because of her good marks she was allowed to go Winnipeg to see her mother, whom she hardly knew. Her mother was apparently unable to provide her with a place to stay, however, and Tina ended up on the street.

Police officers saw her in the company of an older man, but all they did was separate them and leave her on her own. (There was an outstanding missing persons report at the time, but they didn't know about it or take the time to check.)

Later when Tina was found huddled behind a parked car, paramedics took her to hospital because of sores on her legs. But still no one paid enough attention to realize she was the subject of a missing persons report.

From the hospital Tina was taken to a downtown hotel and left on her own. Alone, she ended up with Cormier who, the Crown suspected, used her for sexual gratification and killed her when he found out she was underage and became afraid she would report the statutory rape.

We don't really know that Cormier killed her, but we do know that her life was unbearably sad. On August 17, 2017, her body was found weighted down in the river in Winnipeg.

Cormier was charged after a sting operation which produced statements by him that indicated he killed Tina, but they were not incriminating enough to satisfy the jury of his guilt.

So, what would have been justice for Tina Fontaine?

Ernest Wesley, the current chief of the Wesley division of the Stoney Nakoda people, once asked me, rather contemptuously, "Justice! What is justice?" In a moment of inspiration, I replied, "For me, justice on the Stoney Indian reserve would be every child having a safe, comfortable place to sleep at night."

If I could make the City of Winnipeg or the Government of Canada do the right thing for Tina Fontaine, it would be to build healing lodges all over Winnipeg and all over Canada. The Royal Commission on Aboriginal Peoples made this recommendation in 1996, and the Truth and Reconciliation Commission repeated it in relation to prisons.

The sad story of Tina's life is unfortunately not unusual. As a judge I would receive presentence reports giving the background of Indigenous offenders. Almost all of them contained references to relatives who had died – suicides, murders, car crashes and other alcohol-related accidents, as well as early death from disease, also frequently due to alcohol. The picture of the lives of the Indigenous people that I formed over the years was shameful. When I spoke out against it in my judgments, I was told to go away.

Tina Fontaine suffered emotionally from the violent death of her father. She probably never received any professional counselling that would have helped her to deal with it. During the last days of her life she was hungry, cold and alone. She was 15 years old and had nowhere to go except to the basement suite of a man who probably used her for sexual gratification.

My vision of justice for young people like her would be healing lodges – not big, hospital-like institutions, but little bungalows where elders and recovering alcoholics would live and be available to just talk to young people. They would have bedrooms where young people like Tina would have a warm, comfortable place to sleep and proper food to eat. Pê Sâkâstêw Centre, for example, a federal facility in Mâskwâcîs, Alberta, was purpose-built as a healing lodge, and while its success rate for rehabilitation has varied, it is a culturally sensitive place for convicted offenders to begin rebuilding their lives. Similar places to provide shelter for homeless Indigenous people would be a huge step toward dealing with the dysfunction and the suffering of the Indigenous people.

Critics of my vision will point to the cost to the taxpayers and say it just cannot happen. To them I say that we, the dominant Canadian society, are here because of people like Sir John A. Macdonald, who built the transcontinental railway and opened the country for settlement by our ancestors. In the process he ignored the treaty promises and did extreme harm to the social and family structure of the Indigenous people. These people are still suffering from the damage done to them by the colonialism of our predecessors. We are still enjoying what was taken from them. We have a responsibility to do everything in our power to repair the damage that was done to them.

❖ 22 ❖

DRUG PROHIBITIONS

*Problem drug use is a symptom, not a cause, of per-
sonal and social maladjustment.*
— Johann Hari quoting Shedler and Block (1990)

Drug prohibitions have done inestimable harm to our society
and produced no measurable benefit. They have allowed criminal
cartels to make billions of dollars and become as powerful as the
governments of the countries from which they operate. They have
imprisoned tens of thousands of young people who harmed no
one but themselves, and perhaps did not even harm themselves.

The legalization of marijuana in Canada and some of the u.s.
states is a step in the right direction.

I totally agree with NDP leader Jagmeet Singh, who says we
should decriminalize all illegal drugs. As a former criminal lawyer he saw first-hand how the current justice system is failing.
His position is that we are incarcerating people who don't need to
be imprisoned; that the majority of people struggling with opioid
addiction are also contending with mental health challenges and
poverty; and that we have to recognize that drug addiction is a
community justice problem, not a criminal justice matter.

I often shake my head remembering people I sent to jail who
I now think would have been so much better off with treatment.

One of my favourite colleagues on the bench was Judge Percy
Marshall. He was always cheerful and one of his oft-stated bits
of advice was: "Always speak to the good in a person." A mutual

friend, Judge David Tilley, once told me that Percy could sentence a man to ten years and do it in such a respectful way that the convicted would thank him for the sentence. Even in the years before my Indigenous-related cases changed my mind, Percy's views impressed me.

One case I remember was a man who pleaded guilty to possession of cocaine for the purpose of trafficking. It was a large amount of the drug and the Crown was asking for a sentence of ten years. The accused was an addict and a "mule" who would get only enough money for his involvement to pay for his own use. I didn't want to send him to prison at all, but I knew that if I didn't give him penitentiary time, the Crown would appeal and the Court of Appeal might well give him the ten years the Crown was asking for. So I engaged in a bit of "lower court manipulation." I gave the accused the lowest sentence I thought I could get away with without triggering a Crown appeal. I explained to him that I appreciated that his involvement was a minor one, but due to the amount of the drug, the shortest sentence I could justify was three years. That was the sentence I imposed and he thanked me.

I now think that the sentence was a terrible injustice, although it was probably less than he might otherwise have received. I proudly reported to Percy that I had managed to impose a sentence of three years in such a way that the accused had thanked me. Percy's reply was: "Always speak to the good in a person."

Another case that gives me great satisfaction to this day was that of a young man I will call Joe Smith. He appeared before me in the court in Banff charged with trafficking in cocaine. He looked pale and short of breath and I asked him if he was ill. The Crown prosecutor, a woman who I felt was much too enthusiastic about her job, volunteered that he had asked her what the sentence would be if he just pleaded guilty, and she had told him she would be asking for a sentence of three years in a federal penitentiary. That news was extremely upsetting to the young man.

I advised him that he should speak to the duty counsel and that he might ultimately receive something less than the Crown was asking for. I adjourned the matter, and he was assigned a lawyer and eventually came back for a sentencing hearing. The facts were that he had, on two or three occasions, sold cocaine to undercover police officers. The Crown took the position that he was a mid-level trafficker and the appropriate sentence was three years. The defence argued he was an addict in need of treatment and asked for a sentence of less than two years. If the sentence were less than two years, I could direct that it be served in the community rather than in an institution. The Crown argued that this would be totally inappropriate for the heinous offence of selling cocaine to support his own addiction. I read through a number of precedent cases and determined that a sentence of 18 months would satisfy the Court of Appeal. I imposed that and directed it be served in the community.

A few years later I was at the RCMP Christmas Ball at the Banff Springs Hotel. Clare Jarman came up to me and said there was someone she wanted me to meet. Clare was the probation officer assigned to the courts for all the years I sat in Banff and Canmore. The man she wanted me to meet was Joe Smith. He had successfully completed his sentence, taken prescribed treatment, recovered from his addiction, enrolled in an apprenticeship program and was engaged to be married. His fiancée was with him and he looked like a different person than the man who had appeared in front of me a few years earlier.

He did not appear physically strong, and I am confident that a penitentiary term would have destroyed him. It comforts me to know that what I did in this case had a good result, but I lament the many other cases in which I just "applied the law," and I wonder how many of those people are still in the system.

For some context about drug issues, I recently read *Chasing the Scream: The First and Last Days of the War on Drugs*, by Johann Hari. The book is the culmination of three years of research and the information Hari presents in it about the fallacies of the war on drugs are an extraordinary indictment of the whole concept of drug prohibition. I find it incomprehensible that his information has not resulted in significant change, but I am hopeful that the more it is repeated, the more likely it is that there will be a paradigm change. The balance of this chapter is a compilation of the items I found most powerful in Hari's book.

He begins with the story of Harry Anslinger, the first commissioner of the u.s. Treasury Department's Federal Bureau of Narcotics. The title of the book, *Chasing the Scream*, comes from an incident when Anslinger, at age 12, heard a woman screaming because she was having a bad reaction to drug use. This apparently was the beginning of his lifelong paranoid obsession with eliminating all drug use.

Anslinger became commissioner in 1930 and held the position until 1962. Before he was appointed, his view on "marihuana" was that it was quite harmless, but as commissioner he viciously condemned it. Apparently the reason why he changed his view was that he wanted to increase the power of his department. The prosecution of marijuana users did just that.

Hari describes Anslinger as both racist and dishonest in his position. After alcohol prohibition was repealed, the budget of his bureau had been severely slashed. So in an effort to restore it, Anslinger warned the House Committee on Appropriations that the use of drugs by Mexican immigrants and African Americans posed a danger to white people. He had received 30 reports from scientific experts on the possible dangers of marijuana, 29 of which said it should not be banned. Only one condemned it, and that was the one Anslinger relied on. He subsequently ignored and actively silenced all information to the contrary, including a report by the American Medical Association.

Anslinger's propaganda effort relied heavily on the lurid case of one Victor Licata, a 21-year-old who killed his mother, father, two brothers and a sister with an axe. Anslinger claimed the crimes were a result of cannabis alone and used the story to generate fear about marijuana use. Later it was documented that Licata had serious mental health issues and that the psychiatrists treating him had not even mentioned marijuana use.

The governing legislation Anslinger relied on was the Harrison Narcotics Tax Act of 1914, the first u.s. federal law which controlled opiates. It was primarily a revenue code that required all businesses producing, importing, compounding or distributing opiates and coca products to register and declare all sales. But it also made possession of such drugs without proper authority a criminal offence and moved addiction from a medical concern to a criminal matter.

The Harrison Act tempered this prohibition with an exemption for medical patients who had prescriptions from their doctors for opiates. The Supreme Court of the u.s. upheld this exemption, allowing doctors to give drugs to addicts to relieve the pain of withdrawal. Yet Anslinger's campaign against drugs nevertheless prosecuted 20,000 physicians. Many of their addicted patients who had previously been able to lead productive lives while getting treatment were reduced to homelessness and crime as a result.

One doctor specifically targeted by Anslinger was Edward Huntington Williams, a distinguished authority on opiate addiction who was sympathetic to the plight of addicts and had set up a clinic to help them. One of the patients he wrote a prescription for turned out to be an informer for Anslinger and Edward Williams was charged, convicted and consequently ruined.

Ironically, both Anslinger and Edward Williams believed the chemicals hooked you forever. It's just that for Anslinger that was why you should be shut away forever, while for Edward Williams it was why you should be given the chemicals by doctors forever.

Edward's brother, Henry Smith Williams, was also a physician but initially did not share Edward's sympathetic view. He believed addicts were simply weaklings who should never have been brought into this world. But after seeing his brother destroyed by Anslinger's war on drugs he did his own investigation and came to the conclusion that drug prohibitions were paid for by the Mafia, which wanted to corner the market in the drugs that were being made illegal.

Henry Smith Williams published his conclusions in a book titled *Drug Addicts are Human Beings* (1938). In it he stated: "The United States government, as represented by its [anti-drug officers], ...has become the greatest and most potent maker of criminals in any recent century."

Smith Williams's book also predicted that if the drug war continued there would be a $5-billion drug smuggling industry in the United States within 50 years. And he was right, almost to the exact year. In fact, the drug prohibitions created two crime waves at once: the illegal trafficking itself, and addicts being driven to crime to pay the exorbitant prices charged by the traffickers.

Hari cites a study by Jeffrey Miron of Harvard University which showed that the murder rate has dramatically increased twice in U.S. history and both times were during periods when prohibition was stepped up. The first was from 1920 to 1933, when alcohol was criminalized. The second was from 1970 to 1990, when the "war on drugs" was escalated.

Nobel Prize-winning economist Milton Friedman asserted that by the mid-1980s the drug trade was responsible for an additional 10,000 murders a year in the U.S.

Chasing the Scream also calls out the racialized nature of the war on drugs:

In 1993, in the death throes of apartheid, South Africa imprisoned 853 black men per hundred thousand in population. The United States imprisons 4,919 black men per hundred thousand (versus only 943 white men). So because of the drug war and the way it is enforced, a black man was far more likely to be jailed in the Land of the Free than in the most notorious white supremacist society in the world.

Hari adds that more than half of Americans have broken drug laws, and where a law is that widely violated, you can't possibly enforce it against every offender. The legal system would collapse under the weight of it. So you go after the people who are least able to resist, to argue back, to appeal – the poorest and most disliked groups. In the United States those are black and Hispanic people, with a smattering of poor whites.

Besides the racial aspect, the treatment of people who are imprisoned for drug use can be totally inhumane. I include this story because it demonstrates the extreme injustice arising from prosecutions that I say shouldn't even happen. In a chapter called "State of Shame" Hari tells the horrifying story of a female prisoner placed in a cage in the sun and left there until she died of the heat. Three guards were fired as a result of her death, but no charges were laid and other guards who did nothing to save her are still employed. Hari researched the background of the woman described only as "Prisoner 109416," and found a man named Richard with whom she had had a child. He said she had been abandoned by her mother at age 3 and kicked out of a foster home at 13. She had turned to prostitution and a Hell's Angels bike gang for protection. She had a child with one of the bikers. The child, Eureka, was taken from her by Arizona child welfare authorities. The father killed himself. Then she met Richard and they had a son. Richard had a steady job with a railroad and they planned to settle in Missouri. That might have worked out, but she went back to Arizona to find Eureka and was arrested on an outstanding warrant for 1.5 g of marijuana. That seemed to be the start of a downward spiral of addiction, ending in the Arizona prison where her death was caused by the treatment she received.

Hari includes a chapter on Vancouver physician Gabor Maté, who left family practice to work with addicts and wrote a bestseller called *In the Realm of Hungry Ghosts*. Maté was influenced by a group of American scientists who did a large-scale longitudinal study of what they called "adverse childhood experiences" and concluded that for each traumatic event a child experienced, the child was two to four times more likely to grow up to be an addicted adult. Writes Hari: "[Maté] has shown that the core of addiction doesn't lie in what you swallow or inject – it's in the pain you feel in your head… Yet we have built a system that thinks we will stop addicts by *increasing* their pain." As Maté bluntly put it: "If I had to design a system that was intended to keep people addicted, I'd design exactly the system that we have right now."

Hari gives a great example of the false belief that drugs *cause* addiction. A famous advertisement that ran on U.S. television in the 1980s, paid for by an organization called Partnership for a Drug-Free America, showed a rat licking at a water bottle while a grave voice-over intoned: "Only one drug is so addictive nine out of 10 laboratory rats will use it. And use it. And use it. Until dead. It's called cocaine and it can do the same thing to you."

Well before that U.S. ad campaign, however, a Simon Fraser University psychology professor named Bruce Alexander had already found it curious that the lab rats used in drug studies were invariably kept in bare cages. How could that be a valid modelling of rats' behaviour in their natural habitat, he wondered, and thus of their reaction to various drugs? Alexander designed an experiment he called "Rat Park," a large, varied enclosure with lots of activities for the rats. Water with morphine was available as well as fresh water. The rats didn't take the drugged water, and Alexander's conclusion was that when the rats were happy with their circumstances they didn't want the drugs.

Explains Hari: "It isn't the drug that causes the harmful behaviour – it's the environment. An isolated rat will almost always become a junkie. A rat with a good life almost never will, no matter how many drugs you make available to him. ...[A]ddiction isn't a disease. Addiction is an adaptation. It's not you, it's the cage you live in."

But why do so many renowned drug experts cling to such obviously outmoded models of addictive behaviour? Why do they essentially ignore the findings of the Gabor Matés and Bruce Alexanders and the large longitudinal studies of the influence of "adverse childhood experiences"? These questions drew a blunt answer when Hari asked them of Dr. Carl Hart at Columbia University: "Almost all the funding for research into illegal drugs is provided by governments waging the drug war," Hart replied, "and they only commission research that reinforces the ideas we already have about drugs."

Fortunately not all governments and the scientists they fund are quite so obtuse. Hari points to the success of Portugal. From the fall of its dictatorship in 1974 and on into the 1980s the country had one of the worst heroin problems in the world. They tried criminalization, crackdowns and punishment but the problem kept getting worse. In 1999 the government established an independent commission made up of nine doctors and judges, with an impartial academic researcher as the chair. They were to draw up a comprehensive plan to deal with the drug problem. The panel said drug users should be treated as full members of society instead of cast out as criminals. Decriminalize all drugs and apply the money formerly spent on arresting, trying and punishing addicts to education and helping addicts to recover. In the years since heroin was decriminalized in Portugal, its use has been halved there, while in the US, where the drug war continues, it has doubled.

❖ 23 ❖

SEXUAL OFFENCES

Aboriginal people want a judicial system that recognizes the native way
of life, our own values and beliefs, and not the white man's way of life.
— Elijah Harper, in *Report of the Aboriginal*
Justice Inquiry of Manitoba (1991)

Wikipedia reports that in 2017 when US actor and activist Alyssa Milano tweeted her accusations against Hollywood producer Harvey Weinstein, and encouraged others to use the hashtag #metoo, there were over 200,000 responses by the end of that day and 500,000 by the end of the next day. On Facebook the hashtag was used by more than 4.7 million people in 12 million posts in the first 24 hours.

These numbers don't really prove anything, but they do indicate there is an all-pervasive problem with sexual misconduct in our population. The magnitude of the problem is immeasurable and apparently enormous.

So what do we do about it? The non-Indigenous criminal justice system will say that every one of the transgressors should be charged, convicted and punished. If the number of #metoo tweets in that single day is any indication of the number of incidents of sexual misconduct, then locating, charging and punishing all of the offenders would likely require a huge increase in the whole justice system – more courts, more judges, more prisons.

My attitude on the punishment of offences in general has changed as a result of my efforts to understand the difficulties

Indigenous people have in the mainstream justice system, and this change in attitude applies to sexual offences as well.

I quoted Elijah Harper's comment on Indigenous justice because it is a very succinct statement of a very complicated concept.

The change in my thinking was largely influenced by *Justice on Trial: Report of the Task Force on the Canadian Criminal Justice System and Its Impact on the Indian and Metis People of Alberta*, also referred to as the Cawsey Report (1991). It gives a very basic analysis of the problem, starting with the different worldviews of the non-Indigenous and the Indigenous cultures.

> The problems that Aboriginal people have with the criminal justice system are, to a large extent, a result of the implicit convictions of White society embodied in Canadian law. The end result is a clash of two cultures. For the Aboriginal people of Alberta this results in non-fulfillment and frustration of expectations because the criminal justice system does not embody their implicit convictions about life and existence. (p. 9-1)

> The basic foundations – those rules of a culture that are dominant in the control of the behaviour of the members of a society – are worldview and value constituted. The underlying premises of White society can be articulated as follows: (p. 9-4)

>> God created the universe, the earth, and everything in it and on it.
>> God created humans in his own image and gave them dominion over everything.
>> God had a chosen people that he blessed to show the true way for all others.
>>
>> ...

The earth and everything in and on it is for the benefit of man.

The underlying foundations of Indian/Metis culture can be stated as follows:

The Creator made everybody, as equals, including humans,
     animals, plants, and inorganic life.
Everybody is inter-related with everybody.

...

Man is subordinate to, and a mere part of, creation.

...

This concept of the justice system as reflecting the basic belief system of the culture of the dominant society, in my view, raises a question: If provisions in the Criminal Code are religion based, is their application a denial of religious freedom for those upon whom the Code is imposed who do not share those religious beliefs?

The Cawsey Report goes on to give a good analysis of the basic differences between the two systems (pp. 9-5, 9-6):

Justice and dispute resolution in White society can best be illustrated by a retributive model of justice which includes the following:

Crime is a violation of the state.
The focus is on establishing blame or guilt.
Truth is best found through an adversarial relationship
     between the offender and the state.
Punishment deters and prevents.
Justice is defined by intent and process (right rules).
Community does not play a leading role.
Action revolves around the offender.
Accountability of the offender is put in terms of
     punishment.

Past behaviour is an important factor.

Social stigma of criminal behaviour is almost unremovable.

Remorse, restitution, and forgiveness are not important factors.

Offenders play a passive role depending on proxy professionals.

Justice and dispute resolution in traditional Aboriginal societies can be illustrated by a restorative model of justice which includes the following:

Crime is a violation of one person by another.

The focus is on problem-solving and restoration of harmony.

Dialogue and negotiation are normative.

Restitution and reconciliation are used as a means of restoration.

Justice is right relationship and harmony.

The community acts as a facilitator in the restorative process.

The offender is impressed with the impact of his action on the total order.

The wholistic context of an offence is taken into consideration including moral, social, economic, political and religious and cosmic considerations.

Stigma of offences is removable through conformity.

Remorse, repentance and forgiveness are important factors.

Offenders take an active role in the restorative process.

So, how does all of this apply to sexual offences? There has been some effort over the last 25 years to incorporate restorative concepts into sentencing, but they have been largely restricted to minor offences.

When I was sitting as a judge, I pretty much followed this

trend. When I dealt with a sexual offender whose actions demonstrated an intent to hurt and humiliate his victim, I imposed the longest sentence I could justify. The chapter on Marlon House in *Bad Medicine* is a case in point. When I dealt with less serious sexual offences, I tried to use restorative concepts as much as I could. The case described in chapter 4 of this book is a good example of the application of Indigenous concepts that I used successfully with non-Indigenous people, and in which the victim experienced a significant benefit.

If I had some of the more serious cases to do over again, I think I would deal with them differently – perhaps shorter sentences with periods of probation to follow, with probation orders that would require treatment. I would also consider lengthy pre-sentence adjournments to allow offenders to enrol in treatment programs, and give them assurance that if they show progress in such programs, sentences would be substantially reduced from what they would otherwise be.

I think I can state without fear of contradiction that the most heinous crime of all is the sexual abuse of children, and yet the Indigenous community of Hollow Water concluded that this crime was too serious to be dealt with by way of imprisonment.

Rupert Ross in his book *Returning to the Teachings* tells the story of this community of about 600 people in northern Manitoba that created a healing process that started with a concern about the young people – their level of substance abuse, vandalism, truancy, suicide and violence involving community children. When a number of different social service agencies decided to work together to deal with these problems, they discovered that many of the children came from dysfunctional homes, and that the alcoholism and violence in the homes had its genesis in generations of sexual abuse.

To deal with this problem, the service providers for suicide prevention, substance abuse, mental health, child protection and other issues formed a "Community Holistic Circle Healing" team, and created a program that incorporates Indigenous and non-Indigenous concepts to develop a healing strategy. The team works with victims and victimizers and all others involved to develop a "healing contract," which is similar to the agreement reached in a community justice conference. When an offence is disclosed, the offender is encouraged to enter an immediate guilty plea, and then sentencing is delayed so that the team and those affected can develop the healing contract. The program has enjoyed huge success in restoring the health of the community as a whole. The participation of the offender in this is so vital that the community has concluded that time spent in jail is a detriment to the process.

If any of my readers are thinking that the intergenerational sexual abuse comes from some primitive nature of Indigenous people, I want to state that I absolutely believe it comes from the abuse that occurred in residential schools. What we know about pre-Contact Indigenous society is that it was peaceful and that children were well cared for. Men and women had different roles but were equal in the decision making of the community. There was a balance in their society that did not exist in the male-dominated and often misogynist society of European nations. Most Indigenous nations were matriarchal and women commanded respect. I once asked a lawyer in Ontario if the stories I had heard about the power of the Iroquois women were true. "Oh yeah," he replied. "When you deal with the Mohawk, a deal's not a deal until granny says so." This balance in their society produced an environment that allowed the children to thrive.

The erosion of the position of women, and then the horrors of the residential school system, has damaged the family environment in many Indigenous communities, and it may take several generations to restore it.

I understand that the erosion of the position women enjoyed

in Indigenous society began with the fur traders. They came from male-dominated societies and would only deal with men. The Indian Act was hugely destructive to the status of Indigenous women. It defined an "Indian" as the descendant of a male Indian. Males could marry non-Indians and retain their status. Indian women who married non-Indian men lost their status. This was contrary to most Indigenous cultures which took lineage through the mother.

The status of women generally in Canada has been poor as well. It was only in 1929 that women were determined to be "persons," and this was a ruling of the Judicial Committee of the Privy Council in England. The Supreme Court of Canada had ruled in 1928 that women were not "persons."

This unfortunate disrespect for women, which is at the root of all those #metoo tweets, is a part of our cultural heritage. I believe that instead of charging every violation, much more would be gained from developing education programs that would teach men and women to understand and respect each other, and to restore the balanced family life necessary for raising healthy, well-adjusted children.

Rupert Ross makes a comment in *Dancing with a Ghost* which I believe supports my view that punishment is far less effective than teaching and treatment. He says:

> Virtually every court-ordered psychiatric assessment I have seen, whether it deals with a Native or non-Native offender, concludes that a major contributing cause to the unlawful act was low self-esteem. A multitude of studies point to self-esteem problems as an important source of violence, especially against women and children. The denigration and abuse of others – the demonstration of power over them – is in large part a desperate assertion of self. Most sexual crimes show the same route: the real issue is not sex but power, not

uncontrolled sensuality but the use of force by those so empty of self-esteem that they will do anything to convince others (and themselves) that they are in fact a force to be reckoned with.

I believe that once we understand where the dysfunction originates, we might come to the conclusion that just punishing sexual offenders is in fact punishing the victims of sexual offences, because it would seem that almost all of the offenders were themselves victims of the same kind of abuse.

In "Responding to Sexual Abuse," a training manual for people working with such cases in Indigenous communities, the authors discern a number of patterns of abuse:

> We now know that sexual abuse is often recycled over and over again from abuser to victim, often from one generation to the next. Following are some of the common patterns that occur in cycles of sexual abuse in many aboriginal communities.

1. Child sexual abuse within the family is by far the most common form of sexual abuse in aboriginal communities.
2. Incest is often inter-generational. In other words, a child victim or an adult survivor will often discover that his/her parents or even grandparents were abused *in the same way* when they were children. [Emphasis in original.]
3. If one child in a family has been abused, frequently all the children in the nuclear family, as well as the children of uncles and aunts, have also been abused. Sexual abuse is a *family system disease*. [Emphasis in original.]
4. Much evidence now indicates that abuse entered Aboriginal family systems two to three generations back, possibly as a result of residential school experiences.
5. Many abusers were themselves abused.

6. Women who were abused will often marry abusers and the cycle will continue.
7. Unless treated, male victims will often become abusers of their own children and the children of relatives.
8. Unless effective intervention is introduced, sexual abuse can recur, generation after generation, within a single family.
9. Much of the abuse remains secret, and because the secret is never told, the abuse continues.

The manual also states:

> [The] current legal environment in Canada presents another set of problems for many aboriginal communities. The cultural inclination of most aboriginal communities is to view sexual abuse as a sickness needing healing, and not as a crime that calls for punishment.

What frequently occurs is that, because a family member will not want an abuser to be punished, they will not report incidents to the police. This appears to produce the result that rather than reducing the number of sexual offences through deterrence, the system may be perpetuating the problem by discouraging reporting.

I asked Michael Bopp, one of the authors of the manual, if there were statistics on item 5. He told me that some experts put the incidence of this cycle at as high as 90 to 95 per cent. If this is true, it means that the majority of sexual offenders were also victims of sexual offences.

I say it would be better to treat such offenders as victims rather than punishing them as victimizers.

❖ 24 ❖

ONE SIZE FITS ALL

I believe minimum sentences are wrong because they do not allow
courts to decide who needs incarceration and who doesn't.
— The author

One of my most serious criticisms of the criminal justice system of Canada is the use of minimum sentences.

I had sent too many young people to jail because I was forced to do so by minimum sentences when I believed the much better disposition was through counselling and treatment. In fact, the reason I resigned my appointment as a judge and ran as a candidate in the 2011 federal election was to be able to speak out against the justice bill being proposed at the time by the Harper Conservatives, of which minimum sentences was a component.

I believe minimum sentences are wrong because they do not allow courts to decide who needs incarceration and who doesn't. I believe this is a violation of the constitutional rights of offenders to have their matters determined by an independent tribunal.

I also disagree with sentencing to a fixed term of imprisonment. This assumes that a court can determine how long it will be before a person is reformed. In the case of *R. v. Blanchard*, for example, the accused was sentenced to 14 years for manslaughter, in the beating death of a fellow inmate. When he reached the end of his term he was released in spite of the fact that he presented a known danger, and he did in fact reoffend.

I much prefer the process in Norway, where such an accused

could have been sentenced to a maximum of 21 years and then five-year increments until it was determined he could be safely released.

❖ 25 ❖

SHIFTING FOCUS FROM JUDICIAL SOLUTIONS TO COMMUNITY SOLUTIONS

The greatness of a community is most accurately meas-
ured by the compassionate actions of its members.
— Coretta Scott King

Twenty years ago I had the privilege of introducing Kay Prannis at a restorative justice lecture series. Kay was the restorative justice planner for the State of Minnesota and was recognized as a leading writer and practitioner on restorative justice. The title of her talk was the title I have adopted for this chapter.

The purpose of this chapter is to demonstrate my concept of an alternative to the present system and to use the case of Jian Ghomeshi as an example of the benefits of my alternative.

The criminal justice system we now have costs billions of dollars and does irreparable harm to many who must come before it. If the money and resources of that system, or even a portion of them, were used to help offenders overcome the ignorance and sickness that has them committing offences, it could make our society a better, healthier place to live, both for the offenders and for everyone else.

I suggest we could do this if we changed the focus of our approach and adopted the Indigenous concept of wrongdoing as ignorance in need of teaching or illness in need of healing.

If I were able to make change, I would create a community justice system that would be designed to take the majority of cases we currently call criminal and deal with them as community problems instead.

I believe the recent case of Jian Ghomeshi is a perfect example of the inadequacy of the current criminal justice system and how much better a system with a different focus could be.

Ghomeshi was a talk show host on CBC and an entertainer. His program Q was a popular interview show and he was considered to be something of a spokesperson for the Canadian way of life.

His status was destroyed in October 2014 when he was fired by the CBC over allegations of unacceptable sexual conduct and then charged with sex-related assaults against three women.

After a lengthy and very publicized trial, he was found not guilty. He had the advantage of an extremely capable lawyer who was able to demonstrate inconsistencies in the evidence given by the complainants, to the extent that the trial judge said the evidence was insufficient to allow him to find beyond a reasonable doubt that the offences were proven.

The usual procedure in the criminal justice system is that an individual who is offended by the behaviour of another makes a report to the police. This report is referred to as a "complaint." The police will investigate the complaint and submit a report of that to a Crown prosecutor, possibly recommending that a criminal charge be laid. The prosecutor will review the police report and decide what charge is to be laid and refer it back to the police, who will then swear an "information" – the document that sets out the charges. The subject of this information is now called "the accused." Every charge in the Criminal Code sets out the punishment to which such an accused is liable upon conviction.

Because a conviction will make the accused liable to punishment, there is a whole system of safeguards to protect accused persons against wrongful punishment. These protections are set out in the Canadian Charter of Rights and Freedoms and include the rights to be presumed innocent, to have a lawyer, to remain silent and to have a fair and public hearing by an independent and impartial tribunal.

In Ghomeshi's case, he exercised his right to be presumed innocent, his right to a lawyer, his right to remain silent, his right to a trial and his right to be proven guilty beyond a reasonable doubt.

He was found not guilty, but he was not found innocent. There can be no doubt that something occurred between him and the three complainants that created a serious problem for the complainants. He won. They lost. Nothing was resolved.

The harm done to Canadian society by this case is considerable. There were more than 20 other women who had complaints against Ghomeshi. None of them pressed charges and likely never will, because of what they saw happen to those who did. There are probably a thousand more women who have been victimized by men but who will never be heard, because they see the futility of trying to get closure in the criminal justice system.

The problem is that the system is too focused on the punishment of wrongdoing. The system takes the complaint, decides on a specific charge, and then has the burden of proving that charge beyond a reasonable doubt.

In the "community" justice system I envisage, punishment would not be on the program. The focus would be on resolution. The complainants/applicants would go to a justice coordinator and apply for a resolution hearing. They would tell their story to the coordinator, who would decide whether there was sufficient cause to require a response. The coordinator would only dismiss an application if they were satisfied it was frivolous or vexatious. The emphasis in this system is on encouraging good relations amongst members of the community. The hearing would consist of a facilitated conversation much like an Indigenous healing circle.

In a case like Ghomeshi's, for example, if the women involved had just been able to have the wrongdoer attend a resolution circle, they could have told him how they felt about the way he treated them. He would have had to listen to them and talk about his own feelings in the specific incidents. It is very possible the various sides would have come to an understanding of one another, and that Ghomeshi would have realized the hurt he caused them, acknowledged it and apologized for it, and that might have been all that would have been necessary in order for them to have closure.

I say that the current justice system has tunnel vision. It only looks at the offence and the offender and fails to see the effect the incident has on the whole community. It goes back to the days of the divine right of kings and the theory that every offence was an offence against the king's peace. If an offender cut off his neighbour's arm, the concern was not the poor fellow who lost his arm, but the disturbance of the king's peace.

My system would open its eyes to the whole picture. It would deal not just with the offence and the effect it has had, but also with the effect the entire process of dealing with the offence has had.

❖ 26 ❖

THE TRC

We owe it to each other to build a Canada based on our shared future.
— Justice Murray Sinclair

When I began my quest to understand the plight of the Indigenous offenders who were coming before me in such disproportionate numbers, I found it somewhat difficult to find reliable information.

I had never heard of residential schools and had never taken any interest in Indigenous people. Like most Canadians I had no knowledge of the history that has resulted in their current circumstances.

Then, in 1996, the report of the Royal Commission on Aboriginal Peoples was released and I was delighted to see it. I obtained all five volumes and read them with great interest. I felt huge optimism that this was going to be the beginning of important change. And then it just seemed to disappear.

In 2008, as a result of the Indian Residential Schools Settlement Agreement, the Truth and Reconciliation Commission was established, and in December 2015 its final report was released. I now see this report as creating another possibility of improvement for the Indigenous people of Canada. I believe that if the TRC's "calls to action" in relation to education are acted on, it will make a tremendous difference in the attitude of non-Indigenous people toward Indigenous people.

While I, as a Canadian, would like to think racism is not a

problem in our country, I am becoming more and more convinced that it is. The reason why those in the dominant society don't realize it is that we don't see it and feel it the way those who are the victims of it do.

I think there was a lot in my "pre-conversion" attitude that could properly be described as latent racism. I had a comfortable feeling of superiority. I was better off financially, better educated and enjoyed a generally more comfortable lifestyle. I looked down on Indigenous people because I didn't know any better. I assumed that their meagre existence was their own responsibility. Like most white people, I assumed they just had to catch up in order to be as well off as the rest of us.

As I have said before, these were not consciously formulated thoughts, but when I look back on my early years as a judge, I can see it was pretty much what I was thinking then.

One of the things I think I did right, though it generated complaints to the Judicial Council by the Stoney Chiefs, was the report I wrote in the inquiry into the death of Sherman Labelle (reproduced in the Appendix to this book). I don't think there is any question that I exceeded my jurisdiction as a Provincial Court judge when I made recommendations that included the abolishment of the Department of Indian Affairs (given that a judge presiding at a fatality inquiry is required only to set out the circumstances of the death and make recommendations that might prevent similar deaths). But it all seemed appropriate to me.

Sherman was a young Stoney who hanged himself. He was unfortunately typical of the disproportionate number of Indigenous youth who take their own lives, so I dealt in my report with the national problem as well.

The report was directed, as required, to the Alberta Minister of Justice and Attorney General, but I doubt the minister of the day, John Havelock, ever read it. It did garner some attention, though.

There were a number of newspaper articles about it, my favourite one being the full-page story in the *Washington Post*.

One of my recommendations for preventing suicides was to put an end to the ignorance about Aboriginal people. I had come to the conclusion that the ignorance of the dominant society about Indigenous people creates difficulties for them which are a contributing factor to the depression that leads to so many suicides.

I was therefore delighted when the Truth and Reconciliation Commission made a number of "calls to action" which if carried through would dispel much of the misinformation about Indigenous people – misinformation that I believe contributes to the hardships they experience.

Some of the calls will create information that has not been readily available. I briefly summarize these as follows:

Call 2 re Child Welfare – Publish annual reports on the number of Aboriginal children who are in care compared with non-Aboriginal children.

Call 9 re Education – Publish annual reports comparing funding of education of First Nations children on and off reserves as well as educational and income attainments of Aboriginal peoples in Canada as compared with non-Aboriginal people.

Call 19 re Health – Publish reports on indicators such as infant mortality, maternal health, suicide, mental health, addictions, life expectancy, birthrates, infant and child health issues, chronic diseases, illness and injury incidents, and the availability of appropriate health services.

Call 39 re Justice – Collect and publish data on the criminal victimization of Aboriginal people, including data related to homicide and family violence victimization

Calls 67 to 70 – Museums and archives to provide

accurate information on Aboriginal peoples and to comply with UNDRIP.

Calls 71 to 76 – Gather information about the burial sites of children who died in residential schools and were buried in unmarked graves.

Calls 77 and 78 – Federal government to fund the National Centre for Truth and Reconciliation to collect records relevant to the history and legacy of residential schools and assist communities in producing their own local histories of the schools.

Calls 79 through 83 – Commemoration of Indigenous peoples, including historical sites; erect a monument in Ottawa and in each provincial capital to honour survivors and all the children lost in residential schools.

Other calls will require members of the public, especially those dealing with Indigenous people, to learn about them. I summarize these as follows:

Call 27 – Ensure that lawyers receive appropriate cultural competency training, including the history and legacy of residential schools, the United Nations Declaration on the Rights of Indigenous Peoples (UNDRIP), treaties and Aboriginal rights, Indigenous law and Aboriginal–Crown relations. This will require skills-based training in intercultural competency, conflict resolution, human rights and antiracism.

Call 28 – Require all law students to take a course in Aboriginal people and the law.

Call 57 – All levels of government to provide education to public service employees on the history of Aboriginal peoples.

Call 62 – All levels of government to make age-appropriate curriculum on residential schools, treaties and Aboriginal peoples' historical and contemporary contributions to Canada a mandatory education requirement for kindergarten to Grade 12 students.

Call 63 – Council of Ministers of Education, Canada, to maintain an annual commitment to Aboriginal education issues.

Call 64 – All levels of government that provide public funds to denominational schools to require such schools to provide education on comparative religious studies, which must include segments on Aboriginal spiritual beliefs and practices developed in collaboration with Indigenous elders.

Call 66 – Federal funding for community-based youth organizations to deliver programs on reconciliation.

Calls 84 through 86 – Media support of reconciliation.

Calls 87 through 91 – Acknowledgement of Aboriginal athletes, and funding for the support of Aboriginal athletes and programs.

Call 92 – The corporate sector to adopt UNDRIP and educate management and staff on intercultural competency.

Call 93 – Newcomers to Canada to receive information about the history of the Aboriginal peoples of Canada.

Call 94 – Oath of citizenship to add the words "including treaties with Indigenous peoples" after the words "...observe the laws of Canada."

All of these TRC calls are aimed at making people aware of the plight of the Indigenous people of Canada. I believe they are crucial to reconciliation, and that reconciliation is crucial to our survival as a nation.

The TRC's calls to action on justice issues were a little disappointing to me, because I didn't think they went far enough. I would have liked to have seen them call for repeal of the Criminal Code and replacement of it with a "community" justice code which would replace punitive measures with treatment, restitution and reconciliation, and would only use confinement in prisons as a last resort, and even then not as a punitive measure but only as a necessary step when needed to protect the public from dangerous offenders.

I of course appreciate that commission chair Murray Sinclair had to make recommendations that are possible within the existing system. I, on the other hand, can say anything I want because I am just talking about my dreams – but change often begins with dreams.

In any event, it was my ambition as a judge to reduce the use of imprisonment, and the TRC has echoed my views. Calls to action 31 to 40 are all directed at doing this.

In brief these calls are as follows (I would like to see them all go further than they do and have added my comments in brackets after each of them):

Call 31 – Implement and evaluate community sanctions that will provide realistic alternatives to imprisonment for Aboriginal offenders and respond to the underlying causes of offending.

(I say this should apply to all offenders.)

Call 32 – Amend the Criminal Code to allow trial judges to depart from mandatory minimum sentences and restrictions on the use of conditional sentences.

(I say all mandatory minimums should be eliminated.)

Call 33 – Recognize the need to address and prevent fetal alcohol spectrum disorder.

(For all offenders.)

Call 34 – Reform criminal justice provisions to better address the needs of offenders with FASD.

(For all offenders.)

Call 35 – Create additional Aboriginal healing lodges in the federal correctional system.

(There should be a properly equipped and staffed healing lodge on every reserve in Canada. This was recommended by the Royal Commission on Aboriginal Peoples in 1996.)

Call 36 – Work with Aboriginal communities to provide culturally relevant services to inmates on issues such as substance abuse, family and domestic violence and overcoming the experience of having been sexually abused.

(I agree that culturally appropriate services for Aboriginals are necessary, but I say there should be individually appropriate services for all offenders, and wherever possible these should be administered in a healing lodge setting rather than a prison.)

Call 37 – Provide more support for Aboriginal programming in halfway houses and parole services.

Call 38 – Commit to eliminating the overrepresentation of Aboriginal youth in custody.

(This should apply to all young people.)

Call 40 – Create accessible Aboriginal-specific victim programs and services.

Again I say there should be more help for victims generally. There are many non-Indigenous women who are victims of crime and who need compassionate treatment in order to deal with trauma. In my world we would replace the system that only seeks to convict and punish with a system that seeks to help all concerned deal with the human failings that lead to wrongful behaviour.

The efforts to reduce the use of the imprisonment are going in the right direction, but I say we should be working toward eliminating all prisons, with the exception of detention facilities necessary for the dangerous or incorrigible few.

❖ 27 ❖

FAQ

I talk about the views expressed in this book with anyone who is prepared to listen, and I often encounter angry responses from well-meaning citizens who think my views are dangerous and would leave society unprotected from criminals. In this chapter I set out some of those challenges and give my best answers.

1. What about the Paul Bernardos of this world. Are you going to try and heal them too? Are you going to release them on the public?

There are people who are so damaged and so dangerous that they require life-long restraint in order to protect the public, but they are not as numerous as you may think. I believe the public perception of the people we label as criminals is that they all present a danger to us. In my 33 years as a judge I mostly dealt with disadvantaged people whose offences were the result of poverty and addictions, and their addictions were the result of lives so depressing that they self-medicated with drugs and alcohol.

2. Why has your interest in Indigenous offenders led you to believe that the system should be changed for everyone?

Prior to taking an interest in the Indigenous offenders, I simply treated everyone in an objective manner. I determined facts on the basis of evidence and sentenced on the basis of precedents. When I became the regular judge in the same community, the people started to become real to me, and I became concerned about their disproportionate numbers and wanted to know the reasons why that was so. This led me to underlying causes of the dysfunction in the Indigenous community that produced so many offenders. The understanding I gained about their problems led me to see that the same was true for non-Indigenous offenders as well.

3. What will you do with offenders who deny their guilt and refuse to co-operate in any investigation?

I would allow them counsel, but the truth of allegations against them would be determined by a conferencing method in which all witnesses would be present in the same room and give their account of what they know about a matter. The alleged offender (accused) would be allowed to speak or remain silent, and if he chose not to speak the gathering could draw their own conclusions from that.

4. Do you think this will ever happen?

There will be huge resistance from the legal profession because the current system is lucrative for them, though it is extremely costly and inefficient.

5. What do you do with people like Bernie Madoff, who bilked thousands of people out of their life savings and has no hope of ever making restitution?

I don't know. It might actually be more difficult for him to return to a society where he would be universally hated than it is for him to hide in a prison cell. There are human problems for which there don't seem to be any solutions, but that doesn't mean we shouldn't be looking for them, or that we should stick to using an archaic system that doesn't help anyone.

❖ 28 ❖

CONCLUSION

A significant portion of the earth's population will soon recognize, if they haven't already done so, that humanity is now faced with the stark choice: evolve or die.
— Eckhart Tolle, *A New Earth*

Eckhart Tolle's thesis in *A New Earth* is that humanity must start thinking at a higher level of consciousness in order to survive. I believe this applies to criminal justice as much as to any other aspect of our civilization, and perhaps more so.

If we as a society are prepared to continue spending billions of dollars to vent our anger, hatred and vengeance, we should maintain our criminal justice system just the way it is.

But if we truly want to have a just, peaceful and safe society, we should be looking to a complete change in our approach to dealing with wrongdoing.

The thinking that created our criminal justice system came from the Dark Ages and a culture of cruelty. That same thinking perpetuates the anger and hatred that leads to mass killings. The United States has one of the most punitive justice systems in the world and I say the same attitude that supports their system contributes to the mass shootings which have become an almost common occurrence in that country.

My thinking changed a great deal over the last 25 years. As I got to know Indigenous people, I came to see that their inherent nature is gentle. I saw the brutally violent offences of some of them as a natural result of 150 years of colonial abuse. From this I came to see that most crime is committed as a result of a history of dysfunction.

I believe that the horrendous murder of Tori Stafford was not the result of a free and voluntary decision by Terri-Lynne McClintic. I believe it was the result of the lifetime of abuse she endured and the unfortunate circumstances that led to the murder. I do not believe that other such killings will be prevented by treating her with inhumanity.

The real solution to wrongdoing will come from understanding its causes and dealing with them. It will not come from doing further wrong to the wrongdoer.

I have great admiration and respect for Rev. Dale Lang, Margot Van Sluytman and Annette Stanwick. They have done themselves and humanity a great service. By overcoming their own anger, hatred and need for vengeance, they have reduced the quantum of anger, hatred and vengeance in humanity, and they have healed themselves.

I feel great compassion for Tara McDonald and Rodney Stafford. I watched them in videos. I saw a deadness in their gaze. I believe that deadness comes from their own emotions. They are prisoners of their own refusal to forgive.

Annette Stanwick signed a copy of her book for me with the note "Forgiveness creates miracles and sets you free." I believe she is absolutely right. I believe Tara McDonald and Rodney Stafford could create a miracle for themselves if they could look at all of the abuse Terri-Lynne McClintic suffered, have compassion for her and forgive her.

I believe that if we changed our criminal justice system to one that understood wrongdoers and helped them, that if we just had healing lodges instead of prisons, we could be working thousands of miracles and our society would enjoy extraordinary benefits.

EPILOGUE I

We are still enjoying what our predecessors took from these people.
Justice demands that we repair the harm that they did to them.
— The author

As I was writing this book, I was feeling quite optimistic about the future of Indigenous/non-Indigenous relations in Canada, and then I became totally discouraged by the SNC Lavalin matter.

I want to be proud of my Canada. I cannot be proud of a country that has been established through the atrocities that have been committed against the Indigenous people, unless we are truly working toward reconciliation.

The government of Canada under Prime Minister Stephen Harper seemed to have no interest in repairing the harm done to the Indigenous people of Canada by colonialism.

In September of 2007 Canada, under the Harper government, cast one of just four votes against the United Nations Declaration on the Rights of Indigenous Peoples (UNDRIP). The document is a statement of the collective and individual rights that are necessary for the survival and well-being of Indigenous peoples around the world. It was passed with 144 votes in favour. Joining Canada in dissent were Australia, New Zealand and the United States.

On June 11, 2008, Harper made an official apology for the residential schools, but he was forced to do this as part of the Indian Residential Schools Settlement Agreement.

Then, in September 2009, he said in a speech to the G20 in Pittsburgh: "We also have no history of colonialism. So we have all of the things that many people admire about great powers, but none of the things that threaten or bother them about great powers." The statement demonstrated either his ignorance or his callous disregard for the damage done to Canada's Indigenous people by Canadian colonialism.

In November 2010, his government gave a very limited endorsement of UNDRIP, saying it was aspirational only and not legally binding.

In June 2015 Harper announced that Canada would not adopt and implement UNDRIP as called for by the Truth and Reconciliation Commission.

Four months later the Liberal party under Justin Trudeau won the election and formed the government. This must have been like night turning to day for the Indigenous people of Canada.

Among his first cabinet, Trudeau named Jody Wilson-Raybould as justice minister and Attorney General, probably the highest political honour ever bestowed on an Indigenous woman in Canada.

In commenting on the cabinet appointments, the Chief of the Assembly of First Nations, Perry Bellegarde, said it was a "new era of reconciliation."

In August 2016, Indigenous Affairs Minister Carolyn Bennett announced at the UN that Canada was now a full supporter of UNDRIP.

On September 21, 2017, Prime Minister Trudeau made an address to the General Assembly of the United Nations in which he outlined the problems of Canadian First Nations and stated his resolve to improve their situation.

In April 2017 NDP MP Romeo Saganash tabled Bill C-262, "An Act to Ensure that the Laws of Canada are in Harmony with the United Nations Declaration on the Rights of Indigenous Peoples." The government supported this bill and it was passed by the House of Commons on May 30, 2018. It is now before the Senate, where it is being delayed by Conservative senators. If it is not passed before the next election, it will not become law.

I set out the above because I see the years of Liberal government as a Golden Age of Indigenous advancement in Canada. I see Justin Trudeau as the greatest champion of Indigenous rights since Elijah Harper prevented the Meech Lake Accord.

This Golden Age may have started coming to an end when Wilson-Raybould was removed as justice minister and Attorney General on January 14, 2019. She resigned from the cabinet on February 12, 2019, and was removed from the Liberal caucus on April 2, 2019.

Wilson-Raybould says the problem was caused by undue pressure being put on her to cause the federal Director of Public Prosecutions to enter into a "deferred prosecution agreement" with SNC Lavalin instead of proceeding with corruption charges.

I have listened to the recording of the December 19 conversation between Wilson-Raybould and Privy Council Clerk Michael Wernick a couple of times and I would summarize Wernick's effort as nothing more than a request to talk about the situation. He says the prime minister wanted to be able to say he has done everything he can in relation to possible job losses. Wilson-Raybould says it is a veiled threat. I hear Wernick as doing nothing more than asking her to talk, and Wilson-Raybould as refusing to listen.

This whole scenario demonstrates my thesis that the Canadian justice system is too punishment-oriented. Wilson-Raybould's background includes serving as a prosecutor, and the Director of Public Prosecutions is a prosecutor. Both of them have a predisposition to prosecute. In this regard they are biased decision makers.

In my experience as a judge I would see prosecutors who would take a conciliatory position on prosecutions. They could resolve huge numbers of cases with plea bargains. In my view these were usually very appropriate and they allowed the court dockets to be manageable. There are those who criticize on principle the entire concept of plea bargains, but the fact is that without them the whole system would become gridlocked.

Conversely, there were other Crowns whom I would describe as having a rabid need to prosecute, convict and punish.

A case in point was a matter in which I was assigned to hear a pretrial conference on an environmental matter. A utility company had released noxious chemicals into a mountain stream. The purpose of the conference was to determine whether any admissions could be made, and how many witnesses would be called, so that an estimate of trial time could be made for scheduling purposes. In the course of the conference the defence lawyer volunteered that the company was prepared to spend something like a million dollars on stream rehabilitation and establish a protocol that would prevent similar problems in the future. I suggested to the prosecutor that it was a very reasonable suggestion and she should consider it. She refused and explained that she felt the prosecution was necessary to deter other companies from allowing such things to happen. The prosecution proceeded and the Crown lost at trial. The court found that the spill was an unavoidable accident. So, not only did the prosecutor put the Crown to the expense of running the trial, she potentially lost the advantage of the offer of resolution. I say "potentially" because the company actually went ahead with the rehabilitation and protocol.

Wilson-Raybould talks about prosecutorial independence and her comments have some merit in the present system. I disagree with the concept. Prosecutors are there to prosecute. To allow a prosecutor absolute independence in making the decision to proceed with charges is just as likely to lead to injustice as not.

My entire thesis in this book is that we could improve the justice system by following the example of traditional Indigenous justice. That would mean seeking resolution of conflict through consensus.

I say that the real misfortune in the SNC Lavalin case is that the Indigenous Attorney General and justice minister was not inclined to take an Indigenous approach to the problem.

EPILOGUE II

The fact that this National Inquiry is happening now doesn't
mean that Indigenous Peoples waited this long to speak
up; it means it took this long for Canada to listen.
— National Inquiry into Missing and Murdered
Indigenous Women and Girls: *Reclaiming*
Power and Place, vol. 1a, Introduction

Just when I thought this book was ready to go to the printer, the report of the National Inquiry into Missing and Murdered Indigenous Women and Girls was released (June 3, 2019). The report raises a number of issues on which I want to comment. I see some of it as positive and some of it as unfortunately negative.

I started my quest to understand Indigenous people in the mid-1990s. My proactive efforts to apply my new-found knowledge in my work as a judge and apply the law in a culturally sensitive manner brought me into conflict with the "white establishment." It also earned me a reputation as an advocate for Indigenous people and for the use of their restorative justice concepts.

In my continuing efforts to increase my understanding of their plight I will occasionally read something, or hear a speaker say something, or have a conversation with an Elder that gives a little more insight. This report did that. It speaks of difficulties Indigenous people have with the inadequately funded and culturally insensitive personnel in healthcare, child welfare, education, law enforcement and other aspects of their lives, and how all of this contributes to the vulnerability of the Indigenous women and girls who are murdered or who go missing.

I was critical of the idea of the report when it was announced. It was my view that it would be much better to spend the millions of dollars allocated for the inquiry to hire detectives and retired police officers to solve some of those cases.

I also expected that the inquiry would just deal with stories by the relatives and friends of the murdered and missing women, and that the conclusion would be that the response by law enforcement was inadequate and culturally insensitive. This was part of it, but there was more. The comprehensive description of all of the factors that make women vulnerable was an eye-opener for me. My position prior to reading the summary of the report would have been that it's just poverty that makes them vulnerable. The report has shown me that the poverty is much more than just a lack of cash in their wallets; it is the whole social system that so grinds them down that they don't care about the danger they put themselves in when, say, they accept a ride from a truck driver who could be a predator or stay with a man who could be violent toward them.

Another huge benefit of this report is that there were hundreds of people who were able to tell their story and have it heard. Under the heading of Successes and Challenges of the National Inquiry it says:

> In reflecting on where we are today, the National Inquiry acknowledges that one of its most important successes is how many people came forward to share their truths. Having so many people break the silence has already created a momentum that is building person by person, community by community.

I think this is very true. Since my retirement as a judge I do some speaking at conferences and other public gatherings, and I always like to take questions from the audience. Occasionally someone will get up and talk and talk and talk. There was a time when I would interrupt and ask them: "What is the question?" or "Can you get to the point?" I was well into the second half of my life (assuming I'm not going to live to be much more than a hundred) when I finally realized the power of listening. Such speakers did not want an answer to a question; they just wanted to be heard. Now, if there is sufficient time in the circumstances, I just tell myself that I should shut up and listen. If the speaker goes home with the feeling that I have listened to them, and the whole meeting has listened to them, that may be what makes the whole event worthwhile.

While I see these very positive aspects of the MMIWG inquiry, there are elements which I see as damaging to the advancement of Indigenous women.

One negative aspect of the report is the insistence on the term *genocide*. There is no question that the inquiry is dealing with an extremely horrendous problem, but the use of *genocide* is in my view inappropriate. It is controversial and confrontational. It has become the focus of argument and disagreement and is detracting from what should be the focus of the report, i.e., to describe the problem that exists today and suggest solutions thereto.

The United Nations Convention on the Prevention and Punishment of the Crime of Genocide defines genocide as

> ... acts committed with intent to destroy, in whole or in part, a national, ethnical, racial or religious group, as such:
>
> a) Killing members of the group;
>
> b) Causing serious bodily or mental harm to members of the group;
>
> c) Deliberately inflicting on the group conditions of life calculated to bring about its physical destruction in whole or in part;
>
> d) Imposing measures intended to prevent births within the group;

e) Forcibly transferring children of the group to another group.

The history of Canada's actions qualify under paragraphs (b) (c) and (e). If you consider the deliberate starving of Big Bear's people to force them to sign the treaty, and the number of children who died in residential schools as a result of malnutrition, unacceptable living conditions and maltreatment by staff, Canada also qualifies under paragraph (a). There is no question that the policies and programs of the government of Canada, from before Confederation until the mid-20th century, came well within the UN definition of genocide. However, the genocidal nature of Canada's treatment of Indigenous people ended with the end of compulsory attendance at residential schools in 1948 and with the 1951 amendments to the Indian Act which removed its most draconian provisions.

Even though the removal of Indigenous children was still occurring in the 1960s and later, I do not agree that this was genocidal. It was done not with the intention of destroying the Indigenous people, but with the intention of saving children from what culturally insensitive childcare workers saw as unacceptable living conditions for children.

When I began trying to understand the plight of Indigenous people in the mid-'90s I spoke of their treatment by Canada as "genocide." I was told by my chief judge that doing so could result in a review of my conduct by the Judicial Council and the loss of my judicial appointment. This is typical of the opposition the dominant society in Canada has toward accusations of genocide, even though it is undeniable that it was indeed happening in the 19th and 20th centuries.

I watched an interview with Roméo Dallaire in which he was asked about the inquiry's use of the word *genocide*. Dallaire, as a lieutenant general in the Canadian Forces, had been commander of the United Nations peacekeeping force in Rwanda in 1993–94 and attempted to stop the genocide waged by Hutu extremists against the Tutsi people. He subsequently served in the Canadian Senate and is a senior fellow at the Montreal Institute for Genocide and Human Rights Studies. In the interview he said that the term *genocide* does not fit the MMIWG situation and it would be better described as "systemic racism."

I agree that systemic racism is a much better term, but even that formulation will be difficult for many in the dominant society to understand.

A good example of systemic racism is the treatment of two-spirit people. In Indigenous cultures these were individuals seen to have a spiritual advantage, and they were held in high esteem. In non-Indigenous cultures there was a time when they were prosecuted and imprisoned for sodomy, and they are still the victims of the negative attitude of many heterosexual people. When non-Indigenous people prosecuted or criticized these two-spirit people, it may have had nothing to do with being anti-Indigenous. In the Indigenous system it was good; in the non-Indigenous system it was bad. When the non-Indigenous was applied to the Indigenous it was systemic racism.

The '60s scoop is another example of systemic racism. The child welfare agencies were staffed by non-Indigenous people. They were accustomed to homes with indoor plumbing, central heating, refrigerated food storage and a certain level of cleanliness and nutrition. When they had occasion to visit Indigenous homes which were suffering from significant poverty, they saw the lack of all those things as not being up to their standards. They saw children living in what to them were unacceptable physical circumstances. What they may not have seen was the love and the spirituality and the supportive culture of the families. So they would take those children and place them in homes of more well-to-do non-Indigenous families where the physical circumstances of the children may have been greatly improved, but their overall quality of life may have been greatly reduced. That reduction in quality of life would also apply to the families from whom they were taken. It will be very difficult to have non-Indigenous people accept this as genocide, but some may be able to see it as systemic racism.

I suggest it is better to describe the current situation of the MMIWG as the aftermath of the genocide of the past two centuries. There is no question that the policies and programs of the past have left Indigenous people in the poverty in which they find themselves today. That poverty, both economic and spiritual, has made them vulnerable to predators and has resulted in what may be as many as 4,000 or more unsolved cases of missing and murdered women.

To qualify as genocide there would have to be an intention, on the part of the people doing it, to destroy the group that are the victims. If the people responsible are random predators with no connection to each other, there can be no common intention that would make the result a genocide.

I suggest, with deference to the Indigenous people who have lost their loved ones, that if every one of the missing women could be found and every one of the murders could be solved, we would probably learn that the majority of the victimizers were other Indigenous people.

Statistics from the federal Department of Justice, for example, state that, in 2015, 90 per cent of accused implicated in homicides of Indigenous victims were themselves Indigenous. Two-thirds of those accused of homicides of Indigenous female victims were Indigenous males. It would seem a reasonable corollary that if 90 per cent of the victims of Indigenous people are Indigenous people, then 90 per cent of the murderers of Indigenous people are probably Indigenous people. If the majority of MMIWG are being killed by other Indigenous people, it is just wrong to say this is a Canadian genocide.

But this doesn't mean the Canadian government has no responsibility in the matter. The tremendous dysfunction that characterizes Indigenous communities is the result of the genocidal policies of the past, the ongoing failure of the government to take sufficient measures to change it, and members of agencies such as the police, educators, social workers and childcare workers who are culturally insensitive.

One of the report's comments I found to be most upsetting was: "For some people, fears that contacting the police may lead to involvement with child welfare means that living with violence is a better choice than losing their children." (Executive Summary, p38)

The report ends with 231 recommendations, or "Calls for Justice." There is no question that the plight of Indigenous people presents a very complex set of problems, but I think the effectiveness of the inquiry is lost in its length and repetitiveness.

The first call is for a national action plan to address violence against Indigenous women, and it goes on for over 4,000 words setting out the details of the suggested plan.

The concept of a national action plan is good, but I say it should address the problems of all Indigenous people. I would suggest it should just say: We call for a National Action Plan to improve living conditions of the Indigenous people of Canada so that they enjoy a standard of living commensurate with all other Canadians.

At least 40 of the calls talk about funding. I suggest there should be one call for funding for implementation of the national action plan, and the amount should be in the multi-billions of dollars.

It embarrasses me that I live in a country that has one of the highest standards of living in the world and yet the majority of the people whose ancestors were here first live in poverty. The real test of the will of the dominant society to change the plight of the First Peoples will be the willingness to devote large sums of money to fund necessary programs for housing, education, social programs, policing and economic development.

The recommendations with which I most strongly disagree are number 1.5, which calls for punishment for violence against Indigenous women, and number 5.19, which calls for homicides which involve a pattern of intimate partner violence to be defined as first degree murder.

It makes me very sad when I hear Indigenous people calling for increased penalties. As a non-Indigenous individual who spent his life in criminal justice, 33 years of it as a judge, I became convinced of the futility of the punitive system and embraced the Indigenous principles of teaching and healing. When I hear these calls from Indigenous people, I lament that their true Indigenous nature, which would be seeking healing, teaching and restorative measures, has been corrupted by the domination of the much more cruel non-Indigenous society.

If my presumption that the majority of the victimizers of the MMIWG are Indigenous is valid, then they too are people who have been damaged and wounded by the history of colonialism, and they too require treatment and healing.

There are some justice recommendations in the report which I wholeheartedly support. For example:

5.11 calls for accessibility to meaningful and culturally appropriate justice practices by expanding restorative justice programs and Indigenous People's courts.

5.13 calls for adequately resourcing legal aid programs.

5.14 calls for evaluating the impact of mandatory minimum sentences and over-incarceration of Indigenous women. (Though I say this should apply to Indigenous men as well.)

5.16 calls for community-based and Indigenous specific options
   for sentencing.

These are my positive and negative reactions to the report. I
summarize by saying that there is some good information in the
document, and the inquiry's greatest success was in just enabling
people to be heard. I lament the controversial use of the word
genocide, and overall I think the $92-million would have been bet-
ter spent building healing lodges as recommended by the Report
of the Royal Commission on Aboriginal Peoples in 1996.

ACKNOWLEDGEMENTS

In about 2008 I joined a little group that meets at the Georgetown Inn in Canmore, Alberta. The Inn sports a sign at the front claiming it is one of the "Charming Inns of Alberta." The group calls itself the Georgetown Institute.

I want to acknowledge members of the group: Joost Aalsberg, Paul Carrick, Michelle Dagenais, Sally Guerin, Rick Hester, Peter Nichol, Lawrence Nyman, Brent Pickard, Peter Rollason and especially Dave Palmer, whom I omitted to mention in the acknowledgements to *Bad Judgment*.

The room where we meet, called the Miner's Lamp Pub, is decorated in traditional English pub style, with wooden floors and wooden furniture and an imposing oak bar. The ceilings are white plaster with large wooden beams, the walls are covered in ornate wallpaper, and there is memorabilia everywhere celebrating the history of Canmore as a mining town and as a skiing and mountaineering centre.

There is a framed notice on the wall that reads:

> The Georgetown Institute meets here
> Wednesdays at 5:00pm.
> Visitors always welcome.
> *Imbibo cum a credo forsit*

We think the Latin motto says: "Drinkers with a thinking problem," but there have been Latin scholars visit us who say this is not a very good translation.

There is a little brass plaque on the table in front of the fireplace that says "Reserved: Georgetown Institute, Wednesdays at 5:00 pm." Each of the members of the Institute has a pewter beer stein with his name inscribed on it. These hang over the bar when not in use, and constitute part of the decor. On the ceiling beam over the Institute table we have hung the mug with Ian Lockwood's name. When Ian died a few years ago, we gathered in that room to drink to his memory and hung his stein above our table so that he will be remembered as long as we continue to gather there.

At one of the first meetings I attended, I met Bob Sandford. Bob is now the EPCOR Chair for Water Security at the United Nations University Institute for Water, Environment and Health. He has written many books on the subject of water, climate and the national parks. He welcomed me as a new member and facetiously commented: "It's good to have you join the club, Judge Reilly, but you understand this is a literary group and if you want to be a member you will have to publish."

Me: "I've wanted to write a book, but I just have never gotten down to doing it."

Bob: "What would you write about?"

The facetious nature of the conversation had become serious.

Me: "I would write about my experience as a judge with jurisdiction over the Stoney Nakoda First Nations at Morley, Alberta; the years of conflict that I experienced as a result of my efforts to improve the delivery of justice to the Stoney Nakoda people; and the changes in my thinking about justice as a result of my experience."

Bob: "Why have you not done it?"

Me: "It just seems like such a huge project that I am too overwhelmed by it to even get started."

Bob: "It sounds to me like more than one book. We should talk more about this."

Some days later Bob called me to say his publisher, Don Gorman, was in town and he wanted to introduce us. I met with Bob and Don at Murietta's restaurant in Calgary over a pint of ale. The pints seem to be a necessary stimulant for literary endeavours. I had pretty much the same conversation with Don as I had had with Bob, but Don was a little more insistent.

"We at Rocky Mountain Books would really like to publish anything you write, and I think Bob is right that you are describing several books."

Don then went out to his vehicle and returned with Bob's book *The Weekender Effect*, a small monograph he had written for RMB's "Manifesto" series. These are little hardcover volumes, about 100 pages of about 200 words a page – basically 20,000 word essays.

Don continued: "Just think this size."

Me: "Okay, I can do that."

Don: "Good. Now what part of your ideas will you put into this? Rocky Mountain Books is mostly focused on matters of local interest, so your stories about the Stoneys are what we would be most interested in."

Me: "That seems like a good place to start."

Don: "What would the title be?"

Me: "That's a good question. John Snow took credit for writing *These Mountains Are Our Sacred Places*. Perhaps I could call it *These Mountains Are My Place to Hide from John Snow*."

We chatted for a while about various possible titles, and then:

Don: "How about *Bad Medicine*.

Me: "Oh, that's perfect. Medicine is the term for Native spirituality, and there is so much bad stuff happening out there that *Bad Medicine* is a perfect fit.

Bob: "I am so glad you are going to do this. Now let me give you some advice. Just put everything down that comes into your head; don't try to edit as you go. Don has an editor who will take your rough work and fine tune it. You may not even recognize it, but it will be your writing and he will make it perfect."

Don: "Yes, Joe Wilderson will do the editing. He used to work for Carswell Legal Publications, so he will be totally appropriate for editing your work."

With a title to get me started and the promise of publication when I was finished, I had the motivation to write my first book. I was still working as a supernumerary judge and sitting almost every day, so it wasn't my only endeavour, but within about six months I had a manuscript ready for Joe Wilderson to work on.

Joe was a delight to work with. He would get excited over every story and seemed to just really enjoy his work. He suggested changes and corrected errors in spelling and grammar and rearranged text to make the final product much better than what I had handed him in the beginning.

I thank Don and Bob for getting me started on my fledgling career as a writer, and Bob for his continued pressure to write this book.

There are a number of others I would like to thank as well:

Martin Parnell for his advice to "just do 10 minutes." When it seemed like I couldn't force myself to get writing, that advice was very helpful, and the 10 minutes would sometimes expand to several hours.

My old friend Robert Fulton. Bob is a social worker who has spent most of his career doing research and presenting papers to numerous social service agencies in Ontario. He has shared many insights with me that I have included in this work. After spinning my wheels on this manuscript for several years, I asked him to help me pull my ideas out of the ether and get them on paper. We engaged in lengthy conversations that made it possible for me to do that, and he rewrote some of the chapters, greatly improving them. Without him this might not have been completed for several more years.

Margot Van Sluytman, for her book *Sawbonna: I See You*, and for suggested changes and additions to the chapter on Sawbonna.

Rupert Ross for his books *Dancing With a Ghost* and *Returning to the Teachings* and the many insights they contain.

Thomas King for his book *The Inconvenient Indian*.

Annette Stanwick for *Forgiveness: The Mystery and Miracle.*

Roland Rollinmud for the painting that was reproduced on the cover of each of my books. I have used this as my logo. The symbolism of the feather over the gavel is the Indigenous way taking precedence over the Eurocentric system. The circle of the sweetgrass symbolizes the spirituality of the Indigenous way.

This book is the last instalment of a work I started more than ten years ago. There have been many times when I have had great difficulty in putting words on paper, and I have appreciated gentle encouragement I have received from many friends such as Anne and Garney Baker, Henri and Donna Vultier, Keith Paynter, Helen Diotte, Ron England and Alex Chen, Lorraine England and others too many to mention.

Finally, I wish to give special acknowledgement to my son, Sean Raymond Charles Reilly (born in Calgary, November 11, 1970; died in Taiwan, August 5, 2016). I have a very pleasant memory of us sitting on the patio at Jameson's pub in Calgary while Sean suggested changes to *Bad Medicine.* For his encouragement when I was working on the manuscript for *Bad Judgment* at his home in Taiwan, and his help on the book report I wrote for the *Alberta Law Review*, on Grace Woo's *Ghost Dancing with Colonialism* (Sean explained the term "paradigm" in a way that I could understand). We planned to work on this book during his recovery from chemotherapy, but the cancer metastasized and he died. It has taken me more than two years to get back to it, but I needed to finish it so that I could dedicate it to him.

APPENDIX

REPORT TO THE MINISTRY OF JUSTICE AND ATTORNEY GENERAL PUBLIC INQUIRY UNDER THE FATALITY INQUIRIES ACT

Whereas a Public Inquiry was held at the Provincial Court in the Town of Cochrane on the 26th of February, 1999 (and by adjournment on the 11th of June 1999) before the Honourable John Reilly, a Provincial Court Judge.

A jury was not summoned and an inquiry was held into the death of Sherman Laron Labelle, age 17, of the Stoney Indian reserve, Morley, Alberta, and the following findings were made:

- Date and time of death: May 21, 1998, at approximately 1:00 am
- Place: George and Sheila Labelle residence, Stoney Indian Reserve, Morley, Alberta
- Medical causes of death: asphyxiation due to hanging
- Manner of death: suicidal

CIRCUMSTANCES UNDER WHICH DEATH OCCURRED

[1] Sherman Labelle hanged himself on the Stoney Reserve at Morley on May 21, 1998.

[2] To examine the circumstances of his death I find that I must look at his personal circumstances, his community circumstances and the circumstances of Aboriginal people of Canada generally.

[3] It is only by looking at his death from these three levels

that meaningful recommendations for the prevention of similar deaths can be made.

PERSONAL CIRCUMSTANCES

[4] Sherman was 17 years old. He was born on the Stoney Indian Reserve at Morley, Alberta. His mother died on May 21, 1994. He became a ward of the Director of Child Welfare shortly before his mother's death as a result of her inability to care for him. He had 16 different placements in four years. He had been in treatment programs at Morley and at the Selkirk Healing Centre in Manitoba, but he was said to be resistant to treatment. He had difficulty at school, and because of poor attendance homeschooling had been arranged for him.

[5] On May 17, 1997, he is alleged to have assaulted a man and left him permanently crippled as a result of a blow to the head. Sherman was to go to trial on June 10, 1998, on charges of aggravated assault and it was said that he always experienced anxiety when he had to go to court.

[6] On the night he hanged himself he was drunk. His blood alcohol level was 220 mg in 100 ml of blood.

[7] On that night he hugged his uncle Conal Labelle, told him that he loved him, and then he went outside, stood on a pail, tied his belt around his neck and around the branch of a tree, kicked the pail out from underneath himself, and hanged by his neck until he was dead.

COMMUNITY CIRCUMSTANCES

[8] Sherman Labelle's suicide is only one of a disproportionate number of suicides in his community, and therefore one must look at the circumstances of the community to see his death in perspective.

[9] The Stoney Indian Reserve at Morley is a community of about 3,000 people. It is divided into three bands: the Wesley,

the Chiniki and the Bearspaw. Each band has its own chief and four councillors; one of the Wesley councillors represents a small reserve of about 200 at Big Horn, and one of the Bearspaw councillors represents another small reserve of about 350 at Eden Valley.

[10] A Stoney Tribal Council member in her seventh term testified that she had kept a diary from 1990 to 1998 which showed 120 drug- and alcohol-related deaths, 48 by suicide. In a community of 3,000, 48 deaths in eight years is two per thousand, which is 10 times the national average of 20 per 100,000.

[11] Sherman was said to be resistant to treatment, but the same witness who said this agreed that the mental health and alcohol treatment programs were two of the weakest on the reserve, and she said it was a community problem requiring community solutions.

[12] A Stoney child care worker who dealt with Sherman said his file was disorganized and did not show respect for Sherman. She said he didn't like "white" people telling him about healing, that he needed support he did not get, that when he was in the Selkirk Treatment Centre in Manitoba he went AWOL and he called her, that he was really lonely. She said that in the five years she was with Stoney Child Services she did not get training she asked for, and she felt that proper training was not as available to Stoney child care workers as it is to others in the province. She also said she was among five workers that were let go due to chief and council.

[13] Sherman was in need of appropriate care, but another witness testified that the Stoney Adolescent Treatment Ranch, a facility for the treatment of teenage alcoholism at Morley, was closed two years ago because of allegations of sexual abuse by staff. They were trying to reopen it again but will lose their funding if this is not done by October 1, 1999.

[14] Sherman was said to be having difficulties in school, and

because of absenteeism, homeschooling had been arranged for him. This led me to ask for further information about the school.

[15] A chief who serves on the education committee talked about how the school should have an environment of learning and should involve the parents, but he admitted that the facilities at the Morley school are limited and that he sends all three of his children to off-reserve schools.

[16] The present, newly appointed, superintendent of schools for the Stoney Nation said he was excited about the prospects for the future of the school. He spoke of reopening industrial arts, home ec and music, and he said the computer situation was in a desperate state. He said these programs were discontinued three years ago because of funding cutbacks, but he indicated there were many more people on the payroll than necessary. He also said that the last graduates from the Morley school were 10 to 12 years ago.

[17] Former members of the Nakoda Education Management Team (NEMT) testified that there had been a successful education program from 1992 to 1996 which had in fact produced two graduates in 1993/94, six in 1994/95, and seven in 1995/96. I believe that the testimony of the current superintendent may have been inaccurate because of selective information given to him by the current administration

[18] Witnesses spoke of the other successes the NEMT had in leadership and life skills programs, and a former principal of the high school at Morley said she believed Sherman Labelle would still be alive if he had been able to take the leadership program that had been created by NEMT.

[19] NEMT and its programs were summarily abolished after the election of December 1996. The reason given by the new tribal council was a lack of funding. The former director of adult and post-secondary education said she believed this explanation was a lie, that the funding was obtained through INAC (Indian

and Northern Affairs Canada), HRDC (Human Resources Development Canada) and WOP (Work Opportunities Program), and that the new council simply refused to sign the applications. She suggested, and this was supported by other witnesses, that the real reason the programs were discontinued was to prevent the advancement of Stoney people so that they can be controlled by those in power.

[20] A member of the tribal council spoke of a proposed business development plan that was opposed by "one-man" (a chief) because he did not want to allow the opportunities for employment that it would create. He testified at length as to the repression of Stoney people as a form of control, and said that tribal income is spent on social services, instead of economic development, as part of a deliberate policy of keeping people dependent so they can be controlled. He volunteered his theory that control leads to the depression that leads to suicide.

[21] In June 1997 I made an order directing the chief Crown prosecutor to cause an investigation into social conditions, political corruption and financial mismanagement, because in my view I required this information to consider the circumstances of an Aboriginal offender in order to apply the new sentencing provisions of the Criminal Code, and in particular section 718.2(e)

[22] At that time, I was just concerned about the money that was unavailable for badly needed programs such as alcohol treatment and anger management. I now believe that the situation is far worse than I suspected. I now believe that not only do vested interests divert money that should be going to help the poor members of this reserve, but I also believe that they deliberately sabotage education, health and welfare programs and economic development in order to keep the people uneducated, unwell and unemployed so that they can be dominated and controlled.

[23] I find that the community circumstances that must be

considered as part of the circumstances of Sherman Labelle's death include the following:

1. A lack of adequate treatment programs for mental health and alcohol problems that may have helped him with his difficulties in these areas.
2. A lack of trauma counselling that might have helped him deal with the loss of his mother when he was 14 years old.
3. A school where jobs were given to family members of those in power regardless of qualifications, and teachers and administrators were fired for political reasons, leaving chaos for the students.
4. The conduct of a tribal government that appeared to be deliberately sabotaging education, health and welfare, and economic development in order to keep the people uneducated, unwell and unemployed so that they could be dominated and controlled.

CIRCUMSTANCES OF CANADIAN ABORIGINAL PEOPLE

[24] In *Choosing Life: Special Report on Suicide among Aboriginal People*, the Royal Commission on Aboriginal Peoples says:

> ... the rate of suicide among Aboriginal people in Canada for all age groups is 2 to 3 times higher than the rate among non-Aboriginal people. It is 5 to 6 times higher among Aboriginal youth then among their average non-Aboriginal peers.... (p. 1)

[25] Olive Dickason, in her book *Canada's First Nations*, says the suicide rate among Natives is six times that of the nation as a whole, and she makes the bold statement that "for individuals under 25 it is the highest in the world." (p. 411)

[26] In *Choosing Life* the Royal Commission says at page 2:

After extensive consultation and study, the commissioners have concluded that high rates of suicide and self injury
among Aboriginal people are the result of a complex mix of
social, cultural, economic and psychological dislocations that
flow from the past into the present. The root causes of these
dislocations lie in the history of colonial relations between
Aboriginal peoples and the authorities and settlers that went
on to establish 'Canada' and in the distortion of Aboriginal
lives that resulted from that history.

We have also concluded that suicide is one of a group of
symptoms, ranging from truancy and lawbreaking to alcohol
and drug abuse and family violence, that are in large part
interchangeable as expressions of the burden of loss, grief and
anger experienced by Aboriginal people in Canadian society.

[27] As Sherman Labelle's death is part of a Canada-wide
problem, I find it appropriate to consider the history of this problem and the present-day effects of that history.

[28] The stated policy of the Canadian government, from
before Confederation until the abandonment of the Liberal
White Paper in 1969, was to assimilate the Aboriginal people.
This meant absorbing them into the general population so completely it would be like they had never existed as a people.

... The first prime minister, Sir John A. Macdonald, soon
informed Parliament that it would be Canada's goal "to do
away with the tribal system and assimilate the Indian people
in all respects with the inhabitants of the Dominion." (RCAP
Report, vol. 1, p. 165)

[29] There are those who will say that this is history and the
non-Aboriginal Canadians of today should not be responsible
for the wrongs of our ancestors. To these people I say that we are
still enjoying what our ancestors took from these people, and we

should take responsibility for what they did to these people. We are responsible for what they suffer today if we continue to do nothing about it.

[30] The policy method was to make life as an Indian so miserable that Indians would not want to be Indians.

[31] The policy tools were treaties, Indian Act control, Indian reserves, Indian agents and residential schools.

[32] The policy theory was that Indians would want to leave their old ways and embrace the superior white culture. It was an expression of what by today's standards would be regarded as the worst of bigoted white racism.

[33] While the policy has been officially abandoned, I believe that the processes it set in motion are still working towards the destruction of Indian peoples as people.

[34] The process involved assuming complete control over the lives of Indians through the provisions of the Indian Act and the totalitarian authority of Indian agents; confining them on reserves until they were sufficiently 'civilized' and educated to join mainstream society; taking children from their families and placing them in residential schools which were designed to 'take the Indian out of the Indian child' and transform them into white Christians.

[35] While the policy was unsuccessful, the injury that was done to these people in terms of social, psychological and economic privation remains with them today.

[36] Indians were promised when the treaties were signed that their way of life would be preserved and they would be able to pursue their traditional ways. Treaty 7 was signed with the Stoney, the tribes of the Blackfoot Confederacy and the Tsuu T'ina in 1877. At that time the Indians were stronger than the few whites who were on the prairies. The railway came to Alberta in 1885, soon white settlement meant that the whites outnumbered the Indians and then they began the process of

taking away their freedom and their way of life. In 1885 the spiritual practice called the Sundance was declared criminal, and a pass system was instituted whereby Indians could not leave reserves without a pass from the Indian agent. Parents who did not allow their children to be taken to the residential schools could be charged criminally.

RESERVES

[37] Reserves were intended as holding places where Indians would stay until they were sufficiently educated and Christianized to join 'white' society. I believe that what the white people did not understand is the Aboriginal concept of community. Where the white people emphasize individuality and 'making it on your own', the Aboriginal emphasis is on 'relationship'. The Indian people did not want to leave their communities and embrace white society, so many have been left on reserves which are just holding places, where they have no purpose or future.

INDIAN AGENTS AND INDIAN CHIEFS

[38] Indian agents were used to control the reserve Indians. This colonial practice would involve obtaining the co-operation of one or two families to help control the rest. The co-operation of these families would be obtained by favouring them with extra rations and privileges. The Indian agent had virtually absolute power. He determined who received rations and who did not. A person could not run for chief without his consent. He determined who could leave the reserve and who could not. He had the authority of a judge, so he could charge, hold a trial and punish. No complaints could be taken to Indian Affairs except through the Indian agent, so there was no recourse if he was unfair. During the Second World War, the wives of Canadian soldiers received a spousal benefit. In the case of Aboriginal soldiers, the spousal benefit was paid to the Indian agent; some of

them used it for the benefit of the spouse, and some of them did not. In the latter case there was no remedy.

> ... Under the terms of the Gradual Enfranchisement Act of 1869, traditional Indian governments were replaced by elected chiefs and councillors, and virtually all decisions required the approval of a federally appointed Indian agent and/or the minister responsible for Indian affairs.... (vol. 2, p. 760)

[39] I believe that this extremely autocratic and unfair system of government was the role model for future elected chiefs. When the use of Indian agents was discontinued in the 1960s, the families that had been used to control the others were more powerful because of the favoured position they had enjoyed under the Indian agents. Those who got their clan leader elected chief were able to continue the same colonial method of governance that they had learned from the Indian agent style of governance.

[40] Witnesses at this inquiry spoke of the powerlessness of the people. One said that they have power on one day, election day, and then it is gone for another two years. They spoke of the damage done by 'phoney tribal custom'. This, they explained, was the concept of Indian chiefs, which are not apart of their tradition at all.

[41] This was discussed in the report of the Royal Commission on Aboriginal People:

> Many First Nations interveners spoke of how the Indian Act system of government had eroded traditional systems of accountability, fostered divisions within their communities, and encouraged what amounted to popularity contests. The first past the post system, whereby the greatest number of votes elected a candidate, was seen as a specially problematic. It permitted large families to gain control of the council and shut other families out of the decision-making process. (vol. 2, p. 128)

[42] The effect this has had on their health was also discussed:

> ...Commissioners have concluded that the lack of economic and political control that Aboriginal people continue to endure, both individually and collectively, contributes significantly to their ill health. (vol. 3, p. 199)

RESIDENTIAL SCHOOLS

[43] Although the residential schools were mostly phased out during the 1960s, the horror of them for the Indian people and their continuing effects cannot be overstated. The RCAP Report describes many problems: cruelty, lack of proper nutrition and health care, and poor education.

> The removal of children from their homes and the denial of their identity through attacks on their language and spiritual beliefs were cruel. But these practices were compounded by the too frequent lack of basic care – the failure to provide adequate food, clothing, medical services and a healthful environment, and the failure to ensure that the children were safe from teachers and staff who abused them physically, sexually, and emotionally. In educational terms too, the schools – day and residential – failed dramatically, with participation rates and grade achievement levels lagging far behind those for non-Aboriginal students. (vol. 1, p. 172)
>
> ... Children were frequently beaten severely with whips, rods and fists, chained and shackled, bound hand and foot and locked in closets, basements and bathrooms, and had their heads shaved or hair closely cropped. (vol. 1, p. 352)
>
> ... Badly built, poorly maintained and overcrowded, the schools' deplorable conditions were a dreadful weight that pressed down on the thousands of children who attended them. For many of those children it proved to be a mortal weight. (vol. 1, p. 340)

... no less an authority than Scott [Duncan C. Scott, Department of Indian Affairs, 1879–1932] asserted that, system-wide, "fifty per cent of the children who passed through these schools did not live to benefit from the education which they received therein." (vol. 1, p. 331)

... The system had failed to keep pace with advances in the general field of education, and because the schools were often in isolated locations and generally offered low salaries, the system had been unable to attract qualified staff. ... as late as 1950, "over 40 per cent of the teaching staff had no professional training. Indeed some had not even graduated from high school."... (vol. 1, p. 319–320)

Although the department admitted in the 1970s that the curriculum had not been geared to the children's "sociological needs," it did little to rectify that situation.... (vol. 1, p. 320)

[44] The lingering effect of these schools is the family dysfunction that comes from generations of Indian children being brought up in them and therefore not having the experience of being raised by their own parents, and thus not learning the parenting skills they needed to raise their own children.

INDIAN AND NORTHERN AFFAIRS CANADA

[45] Prior to my study of the Indian question it was my naive view that the purpose of the Department of Indian Affairs was to support and help the Indian people. I am now inclined to believe that the opposite is the case.

[46] There is no question that the department, in its various forms since Confederation, was created to implement Indian policy, and Indian policy was to contain the Indians until they were assimilated into the general population and no longer existed as distinct peoples. While the policy the department was

implementing has officially changed, I believe the processes of paternalism, fostering dependency and discouraging development on reserves so that the people will move off of them are still at work.

> ... the Indian Act was intended to hasten the assimilation, civilization and eventual annihilation of Indian nations as distinct political, social and economic entities. It was not intended as a mechanism for embracing the Indian nations as partners in Confederation or for fulfilling the responsibilities of the treaty relationship. Rather, it focused on containment and disempowerment – not by accident or by ignorance, but as a matter of conscious and explicit policy. The breaking up of Aboriginal and treaty nations into smaller and smaller units was a deliberate step toward assimilation of Aboriginal individuals into the larger society. (RCAP Report, vol. 2, p. 84)
>
> ... The policy of assimilation had its roots in the nineteenth century, when governments in Canada and the United States – motivated by both philanthropic ideals and notions of European cultural and racial superiority – tried, through civilization and enfranchisement legislation, to eliminate distinct Indian status and to blend Indian lands into the general system. Thus, imprinted on the corporate memory of the Indian Affairs department well into this century was the attitude that Indian people required protection because they were inferior – although with proper education and religious instruction, they could be turned into productive members of society.
>
> Such views became deeply rooted in Canadian society as a whole. As the Penner committee on Indian self-government observed in its 1983 report to Parliament, it is only since the mid-1970s that public perceptions have started to shift. Even today many Canadians subscribe to the goals elaborated by Walter Harris; they do not understand why

one sector of Canadian society should have treaties with another. They continue to believe that the solution to land claims and other issues lies in Aboriginal peoples' integration and assimilation into mainstream society. Such views are being rejected explicitly, however, in emerging international legal principles, and assimilation policies have been criticized by major religious institutions. (vol. 2, p. 532)

[47] The Royal Commission, in volume 2 of its report, *Restructuring the Relationship*, confirms that the whole relationship between the federal government and the Aboriginal peoples of Canada needs to be changed.

The commission recommends that:

2.3.45
The government of Canada present legislation to abolish the Department of Indian Affairs and Northern Development and to replace it by two new departments: a Department of Aboriginal Relations and a Department of Indian and Inuit Services. (p. 354)

[48] I find the circumstances of Canadian Aboriginal people generally that should be considered in relation to this death to be as follows:

1. Sherman Labelle was a part of the complex mix of social, cultural, economic and psychological dislocations that are the result of the history of Indian policy in Canada.
2. He suffered the burden of loss, grief and anger experienced by Aboriginal people in Canadian society.
3. His reserve was a place of helplessness and hopelessness that he was unable to leave because of a history of dependence that was imposed on his people.

4. His tribal government was the natural result of the history of colonial relations and colonial control of Aboriginal peoples.
5. His lack of family support was the damage done by the residential school system to traditional family values of his people.
6. The Department of Indian Affairs apparently did nothing about the lack of educational opportunity, the lack of programs for mental health and alcohol treatment, and the abuses of power by his tribal government.

RECOMMENDATIONS TO PREVENT SIMILAR DEATHS

[49] To prevent young Aboriginal people from taking their own lives there must be a commitment to end the tyranny that dominates and destroys their lives.

1. Prosecute crimes against Aboriginal people.

[50] I recommend that the Provincial Department of Justice establish a Special Prosecutions Branch for the Prosecution of Crimes against Aboriginal People.

[51] This branch should employ investigators from each of the Aboriginal language groups in Alberta so that investigations can be done in the language spoken by victims and accused persons.

[52] It should be given a mandate to prosecute all matters from domestic assaults to racketeering, and that mandate should specifically include investigating and prosecuting any allegations of criminal activity within Indian and Northern Affairs Canada and tribal governments.

[53] It should be given unrestricted authority to decide what cases will be dealt with by way of alternative measures and restorative justice procedures and which will be prosecuted pursuant to the Criminal Code.

[54] The evidence at this inquiry indicated a lack of programs, or weak programs, in mental health and alcohol counselling, no

trauma counselling, a lack of facilities at the school, and even that the school gymnasium had been condemned for lack of maintenance. All these problems relate to funding.

[55] When I ordered an investigation in June 1997, one of my concerns was information that $50-million worth of timber had been taken off the reserve in 1995, and yet none of that money was paid to the tribal government and none was available for badly needed programs.

[56] My understanding is that the resources of this reserve are the common property of all the members of this community and yet $50-million worth of these resources were apparently removed with no accounting and no distribution to the general population, and none of it available for education, health and welfare or economic development. In my view this was a crime against the Stoney people, including Sherman Labelle, and nothing has been or is being done about it.

[57] I suggest a Special Prosecutions Branch could begin with this matter.

[58] In response to my order for an investigation, the Minister of Justice and Attorney General was reported to have said that the matter was not his jurisdiction, that it was the jurisdiction of Indian Affairs. If he said this, he was incorrect to the extent that criminal activity anywhere in the province is the jurisdiction of the provincial Minister of Justice.

[59] In his 1996 report the federal Auditor General said that there was $100-million unaccounted for in the Department of Indian Affairs. I believe that when large amounts of money are poorly accounted for, there is a very high risk of theft and fraud. If the Minister of Justice takes the position that it is not his responsibility, this will create a fertile field for corruption.

[60] Further to my order for an investigation, officials in the Department of Indian Affairs made public statements that this was not necessary because there were procedures in place that

would show any problems. In August of 1997 the Stoney Reserve was placed on a remedial management plan, and on September 8, 1997, the regional office of INAC imposed third-party management on the reserve and commissioned a forensic audit on September 17, 1997.

[61] When the audit was complete Indian and Northern Affairs Canada issued edited copies to the Stoney people with a letter from the department which said:

> Certain segments of the final forensic audit report have been omitted in your attached copy. These segments were removed at DIAND's request in some cases to avoid interfering with any ongoing RCMP investigations and in other cases to ensure that the reputations of innocent persons were not inadvertently harmed.

[62] In my view if Indian Affairs has the power to select the portions of this report that are made available to the people affected by it, they also have the power to cover up any wrongdoing in their own department.

[63] I understand that this conflict and confusion in jurisdiction between the provincial and federal departments is a source of serious frustration to Aboriginal people who have grievances in relation to governance.

[64] This difficulty was dealt with in *Justice on Trial: Report of the Task Force on the Criminal Justice System and its Impact on the Indian and Métis People of Alberta*, otherwise known as the Cawsey Report. That report recommended the establishment of an Aboriginal Justice Commission which would have as part of its mandate:

> ... iii) To negotiate a framework agreement between the government of Canada, the government of Alberta, the Indians and the Métis which delineates the jurisdictional and financial

responsibilities of the government of Canada and the government of Alberta toward Indians and Métis with respect to all components of the criminal justice system.

iv) the Aboriginal Justice Commission would employ an Aboriginal Advocate who would accept all complaints against any person or component of the criminal justice system, and who would ensure that all complaints are processed by existing complaint mechanisms in the criminal justice system.... (vol. 1, pt. 10.0, p. 10-4)

[65] In my study of the problems of Aboriginal peoples over the last few years, I am satisfied there is a lack of recourse for them for wrongs committed against them. A large part of this problem is the confusion in federal and provincial jurisdiction. The Aboriginal Justice Commission recommended by Justice Cawsey, which I understand was never implemented, would have gone a long way to alleviating the problem. In my view it is necessary to go further in order to give Aboriginal peoples the "equal protection of the law" to which they're entitled by s. 15 of the Canadian Charter of Rights and Freedoms.

2. Legislate honesty in the public sector.

[66] I recommend that the provincial government enact a statute that makes it an offence for any person who holds an elected position or who is employed in the public sector to make a false public statement.

[67] Such a statute should provide for penalties that include removal from office or employment, and fines in any amount deemed appropriate by a court, and that the court may direct payment of all or a portion of such fines to informants to bring the action.

[68] Further to my order for an investigation in 1997 there were many public statements made by politicians, officials of

INAC and others denying that there was a problem, or indicating that if there was a problem on the Stoney Reserve, it was an exceptional case.

[69] I believe that some of these statements were false, and I believe a large part of the difficulties faced by Aboriginal people in their quest for justice is the false information about them and their problems.

3. Saturate Indian communities with wellness programs.

[70] I recommend that the provincial Department of Health and Welfare unilaterally provide health care workers to reserve communities, and that all non-Aboriginal workers be required to have an Aboriginal person in training for their position with a deadline for that Aboriginal position person to take over the position.

[71] the Royal Commission made this recommendation:

3.3.6
Federal, provincial and territorial governments collaborate with Aboriginal nations or communities, as appropriate, to

a) develop a system of healing centres to provide direct services, referral and access to specialist services;
b) develop a network of healing lodges to provide residential services oriented to family and community healing;
c) develop and operate healing centres and lodges under Aboriginal control;
d) mandate healing centres and lodges to provide integrated health and social services in culturally appropriate forms; and
e) make the service network available to First Nations, Inuit and Métis communities, in rural and urban settings, on an equitable basis. (RCAP Report, vol. 3, p. 633)

[72] The problems of physical and mental health in reserve communities are approaching what will be a national disaster. Whether this is the responsibility of the federal or provincial governments should not slow immediate steps to reverse the downward spiral that is occurring.

4. Support Aboriginal education systems.

[73] I recommend that the provincial government unilaterally provide teachers and support staff to reserve schools to ensure that the standards of education in those schools are equivalent to provincial standards.

[74] Witnesses testified to a number of students transferred from the reserve school to off-reserve schools who were found to be functioning much below the grade level they were said to be.

5. Put an end to the ignorance about Aboriginal people.

[75] I recommend that the Department of Learning create courses in Aboriginal studies that will honestly and accurately tell the story of the history of Aboriginal peoples, their contributions, their worldview, their cultures and the injustices they have suffered, and make these courses a mandatory part of the curriculum at all levels of grade school.

> We emphasize the need to correct erroneous assumptions and to dispel stereotypes that still abound in the minds of many Canadians, distorting their relationships with Aboriginal people. Accurate information about the history and cultures of the Aboriginal peoples and nations, the role of treaties in the formation of Canada, and the distinctive contributions of Aboriginal people to contemporary Canada should form part of every Canadian student's education. (vol. 3, pp. 463–464)

[76] My own experience in this regard is that I was a judge for almost 20 years and knew virtually nothing about these people

although I exercised the power of a judge over them. When Cochrane became a part of the jurisdiction for which I am the resident judge I made a commitment to educate myself about the Stoney people in particular and Aboriginal justice issues in general. What I have learned has been a most troubling lesson, but I firmly believe that if it is not generally known, it will continue, and I do not believe that the people of Canada would allow the plight of the Aboriginal people to continue if only they knew more about it.

6. Support the creation of broad-based First Nation governments.

[77] I recommend that the provincial government provide funding for members of First Nations in Alberta to hold meetings for the purpose of uniting their local communities to form broad-based First Nations governments.

[78] I recommend that the provincial government consider creating electoral districts which would be comprised of groupings of Aboriginal communities so that there would be MLAS elected by an Aboriginal electorate.

[79] The Royal Commission dealt with the distinction between the terms 'First Nation' and 'local community':

> First Nations hold differing views regarding the most appropriate level for governmental institutions. These differences are reflected in the varying ways in which the term First Nation is used. Sometimes it is used in a broad sense to indicate a body of Indian people whose members have a shared sense of national identity based on a common heritage, situation and outlook, including such elements as history, language, culture, spirituality, ancestry and homeland. Under this usage, a First Nation would often be composed of a number of local communities living on distinct territorial bases. However, in other instances the term First Nation is used in

a narrow sense to identify a single local community of Indian people living on its own territorial base, often a reserve governed by the Indian Act. (vol. 2, p. 150)

The Commission considers the right of self-determination to be vested in Aboriginal nations rather than small local communities. By Aboriginal nation we mean a sizable body of Aboriginal people with a shared sense of national identity that constitutes the predominant population in a certain territory or group of territories. There are 60 to 80 historically based nations in Canada at present, comprising a thousand or so local Aboriginal communities. (vol. 2, p. 158)

The Commission recommends that

2.3.7

All governments in Canada recognize that the right of self-government is vested in Aboriginal nations rather than small local communities. (vol. 2, p. 224)

[80] I believe that the formation of First Nations governments in the larger sense described by the Royal Commission would make it more difficult to perpetrate the abuses of power that apparently occur in the small local communities, and the larger nations would have the capacity to create institutions which would be a recourse for members of the local communities.

[81] I believe that if groups of reserve communities were to make up a single electoral district, established political parties would become more active in political activities in those Aboriginal communities and it would both educate the people in relation to real democracy, and give them a voice in government.

7. Support the abolition of Indian and Northern Affairs Canada

[82] I recommend that the provincial government take a position with the federal government that it supports the abolition of INAC and the reallocation of funding that presently is disbursed

by that department to change the power structure of Aboriginal people.

[83] I cannot believe that the abuses of power that have occurred in this tribal government have happened without the knowledge and even the complicity of the officials in the Department of Indian Affairs.

[84] Witnesses at this inquiry spoke of the department being unwilling or unable to help with the problems on the reserve.

[85] The problem of Indian policy was once described to me as a funnel – all the money and power comes through this funnel but most of the money gets stuck in the top of it and never gets to the people for whom it is intended.

[86] I suggest that the Aboriginal people of Canada would be much better off if the federal government abolished the department and all of its programs and paid the money out to Aboriginal families in an amount which, after tax, would give them a living wage. I say after tax because a portion of it should be taxed to First Nations governments so that they could provide services, but it should go to the people first and then from the people to the government so that it is clear that the people have the power.

8. Support economic development in Aboriginal communities.

[87] The Royal Commission says this about economic development:

> Three problems need to be solved to create a safe environment for development. First, a way needs to be found to separate and limit powers. If power is concentrated in a few hands, and if there are few constraints on its exercise, there is a strong risk that those with power will use it in their own interests, possibly at the expense of others in the community. Second, there must be a means to settle disputes that

is open and impartial and provides the assurance of the fair hearing, with judgment rendered by a body not controlled by government or any community faction. Third, a way needs to be found to guard against inappropriate political involvement in the day-to-day decisions of business ventures or economic development institutions. (vol. 2, p. 811)

[88] I believe reserve communities could be valuable economic units that could contribute to the economy of this province. Supporting economic development on reserves would also allow young people the ability to stay in their communities and be employed. There are serious problems that will have to be overcome to do this, but the alternative is the continuing despair of young Aboriginal people.

9. Demand accountability in Aboriginal matters

[89] I recommend that the provincial government demand that the federal government and INAC put strict guidelines on monies paid out, so that they in fact go to the people for whom they are intended.

Governments with the authority and responsibility to spend public funds for particular purposes should be held accountable for such expenditures, primarily by their citizens and also by other governments from which they receive fiscal transfers. In the context of Aboriginal governments, it is our view that this accountability rests with the Aboriginal nation rather than individual communities. Funding arrangements should reflect this basic objective, allowing for processes and systems of accountability that are both explicit and transparent. (vol. 2, p. 268)

[90] At present it is extremely difficult to prosecute fraudulent transactions in Aboriginal matters because there are insufficient

controls and guidelines on how money is to be used. While there are not yet First Nations governments to demand this accountability from local communities, it is all the more necessary that the federal government provide guidelines and controls.

SUMMARY

[91] Suicides amongst Aboriginal people are the result of the history of injustices they have suffered and continued to suffer. In order to prevent similar deaths, the injustices must be eliminated. I have herein set out the first steps that I believe should be taken in this regard.

[92] Finally, I acknowledge the federal government for establishing the Royal Commission on Aboriginal Peoples. The report of this commission is an exhaustive work on the history and condition of the Aboriginal people of Canada and has been of great assistance to me in my efforts to understand the Aboriginal people and Aboriginal justice issues. My only difficulty with the report is that the material becomes buried in its own length. I have herein extracted portions that I believe to be most relevant to the condition of Aboriginal people in relation to the death of Sherman Labelle.

Dated this 16th day of September 1999,

John Reilly P.C.J.

BOOKSHELF

Aboriginal Justice Inquiry Commission. *Report of the Aboriginal Justice Inquiry of Manitoba.* 3 vols. Winnipeg: Government of Manitoba, 1991. Accessed 2019-06-01 (html) from is.gd/GwouET.

Bopp, Judie, and Michael Bopp. "At the Time of Disclosure: A Manual for Front-line Community Workers Dealing with Sexual Abuse Disclosures in Aboriginal Communities." Aboriginal Peoples Collection, Technical Series, Report no. APC-TS-2-CA. Ottawa: Ministry of the Solicitor General, 1997. Accessed 2018-11-30 (pdf) at is.gd/eA7XaD.

———. "Responding to Sexual Abuse: Developing a Community-Based Sexual Abuse Response Team In Aboriginal Communities." Aboriginal Peoples Collection, Technical Series, Report no. APC-TS-1-CA. Ottawa: Ministry of the Solicitor General, 1997. Accessed 2018-11-30 (pdf) at is.gd/QRj49c.

Cawsey, Allan. *Justice on Trial: Report of the Task Force on the Canadian Criminal Justice System and Its Impact on the Indian and Metis People of Alberta.* 3 vols. Edmonton: Aboriginal Affairs and Northern Development, 1991. Accessed 2018-11-30 (non-searchable pdf scans) from is.gd/AISdDb.

Dickason, Olive P. *Canada's First Nations: A History of Founding Peoples from Earliest Times.* 4th ed. Toronto: Oxford University Press, 2009. First published 1992 by McClelland & Stewart.

EchoHawk, Larry. "Justice for Native Americans Requires Returning to Our Constitutional Origins." Review of *Tribes, Treaties, and Constitutional Tribulations,* by Vine Deloria and David Eugene Wilkins (Austin: University of Texas Press, 2001). *Green Bag Review* (2d) 4, no. 1 (Autumn 2000): 101. Non-linked mention in journal issue ToC accessed 2018-11-30 at is.gd/ZyEgLX.

Evans, C.D., and Lorene Shyba. *Tough Crimes: True Cases by Top Canadian Criminal Lawyers.* Calgary: Durance Vile Publications, 2014.

Felitti, Vincent J., et al. "Relationship of Childhood Abuse and Household Dysfunction to Many of the Leading Causes of Death in Adults: The Adverse Childhood Experiences (ACE) Study." *American Journal of Preventive Medicine* 14, no. 4 (May 1, 1998): 245–258. Accessed 2019-05-30 (pdf) at is.gd/3Y8gBW.

Glenn, Jack. *Once Upon an Oldman: Special Interest Politics and the Oldman River Dam.* Vancouver: UBC Press, 1999.

Hari, Johann. *Chasing the Scream: The First and Last Days of the War on Drugs.* New York: Bloomsbury, 2015.

Harper, Hilary, et al. "The Right to be Special: Native Alcohol and Drug Counsellor's Handbook for Working with Sexual Abuse Disclosure." Calgary: National Native Association of Treatment Centre Directors, 1991.

King, Thomas. *The Inconvenient Indian: A Curious Account of Native People in North America.* Toronto: Doubleday Canada, 2012.

Maté, Gabor. *In the Realm of Hungry Ghosts: Close Encounters with Addiction.* Rev. ed. Toronto: Vintage Canada, 2018. First published 2007 by Knopf Canada.

Morris, Ruth. "But What About the Dangerous Few?" Pamphlet, 1994, reprinted in W. Gordon West and Ruth Morris, eds., *The Case for Penal Abolition.* Toronto: Canadian Scholars' Press, 2000.

———. *Stories of Transformative Justice.* Toronto: Canadian Scholars' Press, 2000.

National Inquiry into Missing and Murdered Indigenous Women and Girls. *Reclaiming Power and Place: Final Report.* 2 vols. plus ancillary documents. Ottawa: Government of Canada, 2017. Accessed 2019-05-30 (pdf) from is.gd/Pi97rr.

Paul, Daniel N. *We Were Not the Savages: A Micmac Perspective on the Collision of European and Aboriginal Civilizations.* Halifax: Nimbus, 1993.

Probasco, Robert D. "Indian Tribes, Civil Rights, and Federal Courts." *Texas Wesleyan Law Review* 7 no. 2 (Spring 2001): 119 at 152 (pdf p35). Accessed 2018-11-30 from is.gd/XJTAFr.

Reilly, John. *Bad Judgment: The Myth of First Nations Equality and Judicial Independence in Canada.* Victoria: Rocky Mountain Books, 2014.

———. *Bad Medicine: A Judge's Struggle for Justice in a First Nations Community.* Victoria: Rocky Mountain Books, 2010.

———. "Book Review: *Ghost Dancing with Colonialism: Decolonization and Indigenous Rights at the Supreme Court of Canada*, by Grace Li Xiu Woo (Vancouver: UBC Press, 2011)." *Alberta Law Review* 50, no. 1 (2012): 219–223. Accessed 2019-03-12 (pdf) at doi.org/10.29173/alr277.

———. "Report to the Ministry of Justice and Attorney General on a Public Inquiry under the Fatality Inquiries Act," September 16, 1999. Accessed 2018-11-30 (redacted pdf) at is.gd/ns6nNs.

Ross, Rupert. *Dancing with a Ghost: Exploring Aboriginal Reality.* Toronto: Penguin Canada, 2006. First published Markham, Ont.: Octopus Books, 1992.

———. *Indigenous Healing: Exploring Traditional Paths.* Toronto: Penguin Group, 2014.

———. *Returning to the Teachings: Exploring Aboriginal Justice.* Toronto: Penguin Books, 1996; 2nd ed. with a new introduction, 2006.

———. "Walking the Traditional Paths: Uncovering the Gateway to Indigenous Healing in the Justice System." *Justice as Healing: A Newsletter on Aboriginal Concepts of Justice* 19, no. 3 (2014): 1–7. Accessed 2018-11-30 (pdf) at commentary.canlii.org/w/canlii/2014CanLIIDocs6.pdf.

Royal Commission on Aboriginal Peoples (RCAP). *Bridging the Cultural Divide: A Report on Aboriginal People and Criminal Justice in Canada.* Ottawa: Canada Communication Group, 1996. Accessed 2018-11-30 (pdf) from is.gd/gDDwlo.

———. *Choosing Life: Special Report on Suicide among Aboriginal People.* Ottawa: Canada Communication Group, 1995. Accessed 2018-11-30 (pdf) from is.gd/9UNeJj.

———. *Report of the Royal Commission on Aboriginal Peoples.* 5 vols. Ottawa: Canada Communication Group, 1996. Accessed 2018-11-30 (pdf) from is.gd/Y1SepA.

Saul, John Ralston. *A Fair Country: Telling Truths about Canada.* Toronto: Viking Canada, 2008.

Sgroi, Suzanne M. *Handbook of Clinical Interventions in Child Sexual Abuse.* Lexington, Mass.: Lexington Books, 1981, 1990.

Shedler, J., and J. Block. "Adolescent drug use and psychological health. A longitudinal inquiry." *The American Psychologist* 45, no. 5 (May 1990): 612–630. Accessed 2018-11-30 (abstract only) at is.gd/uzbDj2.

Sherman, Lawrence W. "Domestic Violence and Defiance Theory: Understanding Why Arrest Can Backfire." In Duncan Chappell and Sandra Egger, eds., *Australian Violence: Contemporary Perspectives II*, 207–220. Canberra: Australian Institute of Criminology, 1995. Accessed 2018-11-30 (pdf pp243–256) from aic.gov.au/node/5864.

Silver, Lisa A. "Unpacking *R. v. Barton* [2017 ABCA 216]." *ABlawg* (University of Calgary Faculty of Law blog), July 27, 2017. Accessed 2018-11-30 at ablawg.ca/?p=8763.

Stanwick, Annette. *Forgiveness: The Mystery and Miracle: Finding Freedom and Peace at Last.* Calgary: Heart Message Publishing, 2007.

Tolle, Eckhart. *A New Earth: Awakening to Your Life's Purpose*. New York: Plume 2005, 2016.

Truth and Reconciliation Commission of Canada. *Honouring the Truth, Reconciling for the Future: Summary of the Final Report*. Accessed 2018-11-30 (pdf) at is.gd/9hMvB2.

United Nations Convention on the Prevention and Punishment of the Crime of Genocide. General Assembly Resolution 260A (III) (December 9, 1948); in force as of January 12, 1951, in accordance with art. XIII. Accessed 2019-06-01 (pdf) from is.gd/YaUB95.

Van Sluytman, Margot. *Sawbonna: I See You: A Real Life Restorative Justice Story*. Calgary: Palabras Press, 2009.

Williams, Henry Smith. *Drug Addicts Are Human Beings: The Story of Our Billion-Dollar Drug Racket, How We Created It and How We Can Wipe It Out*. Washington, DC: Shaw Publishing, 1938.

CASES

Crow Dog v. Spotted Tail. See *Ex parte Crow Dog*.

Edwards v. Canada (Attorney General), 1929 CanLII 438 (UK JCPC). Accessed 2018-11-30 at canlii.ca/t/gbvs4.

Ex parte Crow Dog, 109 U.S. 556 (1883) (U.S. Supreme Court). Accessed 2018-11-30 from is.gd/hYbVgg.

R. v. Barton, 2011 ABQB 492. [Application for judicial interim release pending trial.] Accessed 2018-11-30 at canlii.ca/t/gmldr.

R. v. Barton, 2013 ABQB 673. [*Voir dire* on Charter breach.] Accessed 2018-11-30 at canlii.ca/t/gkgm2.

R. v. Barton, 2015 ABQB 159. [*Voir dire* on admissibility of autopsy tissue evidence.] Accessed 2018-11-30 at canlii.ca/t/gj0x3.

R. v. Barton, 2017 ABCA 216. [Appeal from 2015 acquittal.] Accessed 2018-11-30 at canlii.ca/t/h4l2o.

R. v. Blanchard, 2016 ABQB 520. [Macklin J. on *Mills* application #1.] Accessed 2018-11-30 at canlii.ca/t/gwk56.

R. v. Blanchard, 2017 ABQB 369. [Macklin J. on stay application.] Accessed 2018-11-30 at canlii.ca/t/h47ov.

R. v. Gladue, 1999 CanLII 679 (SCC). Accessed 2018-11-30 at canlii.ca/t/1fqp2.

R. v. Wagar, 2015 ABCA 327. Accessed 2018-12-01 at canlii.ca/t/gls9m.

R. v. Wagar, 2017 ABPC 17. [Retrial.] Accessed 2018-12-01 at canlii.ca/t/gxdc5.

Section 24 of the BNA Act, Re. See *Edwards v. Canada.*

STATUTES

Constitution Act, 1982, Schedule B to the Canada Act 1982 (UK), 1982, c. 11. Accessed 2018-11-30 at canlii.ca/t/ldsx.

Criminal Code, R.S.C. 1985, c. C-46, s. 718.2. Accessed 2018-11-30 at canlii.ca/t/53jff#sec718.2.

INDEX OF NAMES